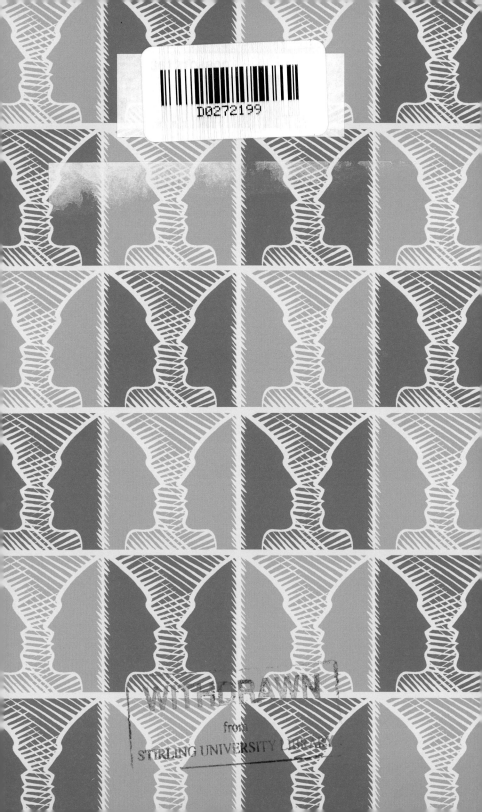

In Cold Ink

David Robinson

ON THE WRITERS' TRACKS

Maclean Dubois

First Published in Great Britain in 2008 by Maclean Dubois
Hillend House, Hillend, Edinburgh EH10 7DX

Copyright © by David Robinson 2008
The moral right of the author has been asserted
ISBN 978-0-9514470-5-5

Printed by Cromwell Press www.cromwellpres.co.uk
Distributed by Birlinn Ltd
Design by Cate Stewart

Photographs of the authors by kind permission from
www.writerpictures.com
Willy Russell by Pascal Suez
Bernard MacLaverty by Alex Hewitt
Valerie Martin by Pascal Suez
AL Kennedy by Graham Jepson
Robin Jenkins by Stephen Mansfield/TSPL
Ian McEwan by Graham Jepson
Janice Galloway by Graham Jepson
William Dalrymple by Angus Bremner
William Boyd by Angus Bremner
Zoe Wicomb by Alex Hewitt
David Mitchell by James Emmett
JG Ballard by Graham Jepson
Yiyun Li by Writer Pictures
Tobias Wolff by Graham Jepson
Richard Ford by Riccardo de Luca
Kate Atkinson by Geraint Lewis
Ali Smith by Antonietta Lunesu
Jackie Kay by Walter Neilson
Edwin Morgan by Alex Hewitt
Studs Terkel by David Cruickshanks

This book is dedicated to Jim and Ann Ahern

ACKNOWLEDGEMENTS

Most of these articles have appeared in some form or another in *The Scotsman* and I am grateful to its Editor, Mike Gilson, for allowing me to publish them in book form. I'd also like to thank Alex Hewitt and Writer Pictures for providing the photos; Samantha Kelly for her assiduous editing; Jan Rutherford for her encouragement; Iain McIntosh for his artwork; Cate Stewart for the elegance of her design work, and Lesley Winton for keeping the project on track. I am further, and more generally, indebted to the friendship of Catherine Lockerbie, Lee Randall and Stuart Kelly. Any mistakes in this book are, however, entirely my own work.

Most of all, though, I'd like to thank Alexander McCall Smith, almost certainly the planet's kindest best-selling writer, without whom the book you are holding would be a small log.

Foreword

EVERY August, for seventeen days, my job becomes almost indecently enjoyable. As soon as the world's biggest book festival pitches up in Edinburgh's Charlotte Square, I'm given carte blanche to see as many of the six hundred or so attending writers as I want. Book festivals are a cultural phenomenon of our age – almost every week, it seems, there's one going on somewhere – and the best of them all have one thing in common: the more events you see, the more you become aware of the hidden links that underpin literary culture.

During those August days, I – briefly – become more intelligent, more culturally aware and more sensitive to a whole range of issues. Best of all, I like to see writers whose work is new to me, and as I move from tent to tent, picking up the condensed version of each author's truth, I notice resonances that wouldn't have registered before, parallels and paradoxes to which I would otherwise have been blind. Edinburgh's reputation as the best, as well as the biggest, of the world's book festivals is largely due to the way in which its programme is carefully structured to signpost those intellectual journeys, although mapping your own pathway through it can be just as rewarding.

What I hope for this book of interviews is that it gives readers something similar to a book festival: that each encounter offers something interesting, not only in itself, but also through juxtaposition with the voices around it. If you want to go along with my arrangement, and read the pieces in the sequence I've chosen, then a number of links and contrasts should become apparent: reflections on life and work, on history and conflict, on love and language, on the craft of writing and the difficulties of fame. But plot your own route through the book, and the dialogue between the authors' work might be even more revealing. Like the programmer of a good book festival, I've tried to offer a satisfyingly wide mix: not just world-famous names such as Ian McEwan and Richard Ford but also writers like Yiyun Li and Zoë Wicomb, who deserve a wider audience. In this context, allow me to pass on, as a seasoned book festival-goer, one piece of advice: the biggest discoveries are invariably made in the smallest venues.

Often it's only in the last stages of assembling a book that you start to see the patterns within it. On a personal level, looking back over these interviews has made me realise just how strongly I am drawn to stories of ordinary people whose lives are somehow over-shadowed by best-selling books. In Kansas, I spent time with two families whose lives were affected by Truman Capote's researches for his masterpiece *In Cold Blood;* in Amsterdam I got to know Anne Frank's best friend. My journey along the blurred boundary between life and literature even led to Botswana where, on the trail of the No. 1 Ladies' Detective Agency, I discovered more truth than I had bargained for.

As I type that last globe-trotting paragraph, I am reminded again what a huge privilege and pleasure my job is. I've been a news-paper journalist all my working life, and for the last eight years, as books editor of *The Scotsman,* I've had the chance to meet people whose work I admire, love or – as in the case of veteran Chicagoan journalist Studs Terkel – just plain idolise. For me, Terkel is the greatest of all interviewers, which is why I end this book with my own, slightly surreal, interview with him. He knows that he himself isn't the story, but the people he is talking to are, so he doesn't put himself unnecessarily in the picture, bask in the reflected light of celebrity or abuse the interviewer's unfair advantage of always having the last word. A Terkel interview, therefore, is completely transparent. It's not distorted by ego, but is a genuine attempt to understand more about his interviewees, and to help them explain their ideas. The way I see it, my job is the same – though a lot more straightforward, because authors are probably the easiest people on the planet to interview. Not only that but, since language is their medium, they tend to be disproportionately eloquent about it too.

I'd like to thank all of the writers who have allowed me to interview them, and also *The Scotsman,* in which versions of most of these pieces first appeared. The biggest thanks of all, though, must go to Alexander McCall Smith, who first suggested publishing this book.

A few years ago, Margaret Atwood told me what it felt like to be the object of an interviewer's attentions. "With some interviews," she said, "it can feel like an effortless glide round the ballroom; with others it's just an embarrassed shuffle where you're not sure who's leading whom. Then you get a third type, and they're the really dangerous ones. You're gliding round the ballroom, then the music comes to an end and, quite coolly and deliberately, they take aim and kick you in the shins or stamp on your toes."

It's not always been an effortless glide, but I think I've stayed clear of shins and toes. I've certainly enjoyed the dance, and I hope you, the reader, will too.

Looking For Truman Capote

THE BEST time and place I can think of to begin this book is 18 September 2007, in Kansas. I am driving west, alone in a hired car. An unconvincing audiobook dramatisation of *Wuthering Heights* is playing on the stereo: something I brought along for the ride because I'm a newspaper's books editor and there are whole stacks of books, including an embarrassing number of classics, that I really should have read by now. As I grew up only ten miles from the barren moors on which Heathcliff was first found, the Brontës are one of my deepest, most shaming pools of ignorance.

So I'm a stranger in this vast, open country, and the ancient seabed I'm driving across — those enormous plains that stretch a thousand miles to the south and two thousand to the north — is the most humbling landscape I have seen. Yet at the same time it's refreshing; energising. If you're from a narrow, hilly, European island, it's impossible to feel jaded driving to west Kansas. Because the land is so flat, sunrise and sunset can last for hours. Because the skies between them are so huge, you feel exposed, stripped down, small. Small, and scurrying across a 360-degree prairie in a hired car, trying and failing to take in Emily Brontë's now alien-sounding, convoluted tale.

I drive through Greensburg where, six months before, a tornado ripped through a town of 1,500 people, killing twelve of them and wiping away 95% of the houses. It was probably a couple of paragraphs in the newspapers back home in Scotland, but when you drive through a town whose streets have been emptied of everything apart from grass and tarmac, a mere twelve deaths seems a minor miracle. Extreme weather stories make compelling TV news, but after a while, they start to fog up the mind. Some things can unfog it pretty damn quick though, like the first time you see a tree trunk, six foot thick, snapped through by a tornado. If you want to check the difference between reality and what you imagine reality to be, a before-your-very-eyes snapped-through Greensburg elm does the job as well as anything.

Stopping the car in front of the shattered elm, I got out. Around me was a vanished suburbia; the grid patterns of roads the only remaining clue. Up ahead on the main road to Dodge City, a tented field hospital had been erected to look after those injured on 4 May 2007 when, around nightfall, a tornado over a mile and a half wide suddenly swept out of a wall of rain and vacuumed up the main street. Now, bulldozers and cranes were at work, slowly putting the few houses not completely obliterated back together again. Somewhere around here, a Scottish tabloid journalist I'd spent the last few days with was talking to some of the other tornado survivors, writing a nice colour piece about how they were reassembling their lives and mourning those gone with the wind.

I don't mean to mock. I'm a journalist, have been one all my working life, and I know what the pull of a news story is, even though I've grown more immune to it over the years. But hanging around Greensburg for longer than it took to stare at that broken elm just felt wrong. Squinting through the lens of my disposable camera, I took a picture of the sundered tree, got back in the car again, and headed west, across the rain-fingered plains to Garden City. Something deeper than a news story was pulling me there. It'll take some explaining.

In the rest of this book, there will be interviews with authors I've met as part of my job at *The Scotsman*. In its long history, my newspaper has had almost as many kinds of people in charge of dealing with books as there are types of books themselves. I feel awkward comparing myself with them – after all, the novels of the Brontës aren't the only lacunae in my literary education: there are quite a few more that I'm not planning on owning up to for a long while yet. Perhaps it's easier to say what kind of books editor I'm not. I'm not the kind who thinks that their opinion alone matters;

who would happily draw up lists of canonical works and sneer at readers of anything else – and nor do I have a great theory of literary criticism to expound at all costs. Similarly, if I interview an author, I won't let my own opinions get in the way of what he or she is talking about; and I won't try to have the last word, or to be anything other than as transparent as possible. In fact, I'd even go further. Many of the authors I most respect say that their best work happens when their own ego shuts down entirely. I think the same thing can happen in journalism too.

So it's all the odder, as I slip back into gear on the road to Garden City, that the person I'm in search of, whose shadow I am trying to catch, whose book was the last one I ever read to my son as a bedtime story, and the one which still obsesses me above all others, was one of the greatest egotists of the last century.

Truman Capote. By now, you may have guessed the name of the book we're talking about. *In Cold Blood.*

I'm heading towards that book now, getting nearer to it with each wide-open mile. And as I drive towards the town where Capote first came to write up the story, I feel as though all my senses are alert, hungry. I want to know everything about Garden City, about the people I'll meet there – people who knew Capote when he was working on that story with his childhood friend Harper Lee. Tell me the rainfall statistics, the crop rotation patterns, the voting habits of the local county and the state, and my eyes won't glaze over. The average incomes, the prevalence of gangs, the patterns of crime, the kind of churches most people go to, and I won't be feigning interest. Show me the photos, the family albums, what people looked like back in November 1959, and I won't be suppressing a yawn or looking discreetly at my watch. Tell me, quietly, about the secrets: about how there used to be a ban on Negroes and Mexicans at the open air swimming pool; about what it must be like to be gay in such a place as this. Try me on small-town gossip: I'll listen. Most of all, tell me about the Clutter family; about all four of them, who were murdered in cold blood on 16 November, 1959 by two men – Dick Hickock and Perry Smith – who, for their troubles, got away with just $40, a radio and a pair of binoculars.

I'm not an obsessive by nature, but there's something about the way *In Cold Blood* is written that takes it deeper into my mind than any other book. I guess most journalists probably read it and think, like me, "Yes – *that's* the way we should always be writing stories: from the inside." And we know that we hardly ever do, and we understand all the reasons why: the dull pull of deadlines, the cold, dead hand of newspaper style, the fact that we don't all work for the *New Yorker* like Truman Capote, and we don't have either the time or the money to take two months off, head for the scene of a small-town multiple murder, and wander around it for weeks on end until we've found out everything we need to know. We don't have research assistants – and if we did, their name wouldn't be Harper Lee, and they wouldn't have just handed in the best novel of the decade before deciding to join us on a jolly jaunt to a place that was, as Capote later wrote, "as foreign to me as Peking".

The first time I read *In Cold Blood,* I was at university. A serious history student at Oxford looking, as Capote intended, at an ultra-serious question: what makes people kill? But the next time, I was a journalist, had already lost some of that earnestness, and was pre-occupied with other questions – such as how, exactly, Capote had been able to persuade the police chief hunting the murderers to tell him about the dream his wife had about meeting one of the victims. The third time I read it, as a books editor, I was more interested in Capote's style: not just the subtle layering of the story, but how he took all the newspaper clichés he could find – our stereotypical image of murderers, for example – and fed them straight into the shredder.

Even then I didn't notice everything. Reading it yet again as a bedtime story to my son (he was, I should have added, fourteen, and thought the book completely "cool"), I was brought up short by the key moment when Truman Capote sees the two murderers for the first time. Both of the recent Hollywood films about Capote working on *In Cold Blood** have exactly the same scene, so you know it's central. Capote and Harper Lee are on the steps of the Garden City courthouse, along with a small crowd, which has been waiting there a couple of hours for their first glimpse of the killers. Finally, the police cars arrive and the prisoners are led up the steps. One of them – Perry Smith – looks at Capote intently as he is hustled up towards the courthouse jail. The camera dwells on Capote's face, and with hindsight that casual glance becomes weighted with significance. Later, something would happen between those two men: a love affair, an infatuation, a deep identification with each other, a cynical exploitation – take your pick. But it started with that look.

In the book, you don't get a sense of this at all. Instead, the scene begins with a description of two mangy cats prowling around the main Garden City hotel. You wonder what on earth Capote is doing. The answer is: he's not rushing us. He explains that the cats always prowled round the hotel because there they'd find cars that had driven, like mine, hundreds of miles across the high prairie. The cats were checking out the cars for the dead, broken bodies of birds trapped in the radiator grilles. So by the time the crowd has assembled (not a lynch mob, as the local newspaper had pretended to fear – another cliché slapped down – but an amiable, good-humoured gathering) and the murderers have been dragged up the steps in chains past them, that's the image that stays with us: broken, hunted creatures, not automatically guilty men. Only after they've gone into the courthouse do you realise that Capote hasn't given the slightest description of Dick Hickock or Perry Smith. He's smuggled them past our moral attentiveness: he doesn't want us to judge them just yet.

❖   ❖   ❖

My son is in his bed, and I am reading to him as I've done,

*Capote (2005) and *Infamous* (2006)

almost every night, for twelve years. We reach the end of that chapter, and I read the last paragraph twice:

*"No-one lingered, neither the press corps nor any of the townspeople. Warm
rooms and warm suppers beckoned them, and as they hurried away, leaving
the cold square to two grey cats, the miraculous autumn departed too; the
year's first snow began to fall."*

The one definition of journalism that's stuck in my mind the
longest is the one Nicholas Tomalin coined, around the time I was
at university. "All that's needed for success in journalism," he said,
"is ratlike cunning, a plausible manner, and a little literary ability."
That scene with the Garden City cats will do nicely for the literary
ability, and the ratlike cunning is evident throughout Capote's
career. Probably the best example happened two years before
Capote himself drove west across Kansas to Garden City to write
about the Clutter family's murder. In 1957, he flew to Kyoto in
search of an interview with Marlon Brando, who was in Japan to
film *Sayonara*. Brando hardly ever gave interviews, but he talked to
Capote in his hotel room because, after all, they were two famous
Americans in a strange city. And in any case, Capote seemed harm-
less: he certainly wasn't taking any notes.

For five hours, they talked. Capote knew Brando's mother had
been an alcoholic, so he told him all about his own mother's drink
problem. It worked: Brando opened up about the emotional scars
this had left on him, including an inability to feel either love or
trust. *"The secret to the art of interviewing – and it is an art,"* Capote
later wrote, *"is to let the other person think they're interviewing you. You
tell them about yourself, and slowly you spin your web so that he tells you
everything. That's how I trapped Marlon."* In his first interviews with the
Clutter family's killers in Kansas State Penitentiary – where he
established the kind of deep friendship with Perry Smith that gives
the book its special insight into the mind of a murderer – something
similar clearly happened. Later on, when he needed the murderers
to be executed so he could finally have an ending to his book, he had

to pretend to them that he was doing his level best to save them from the noose. If there's any cold blood here, it's the blood in Capote's own heart.

As a journalist, I can't claim Capote's literary ability, and as a books editor I find that ratlike cunning just doesn't come into it: most writers, cooped up with their computer for far too long, will quite happily talk to anyone who asks them what they've been doing. But as I drive ever nearer to Garden City, I can console myself by thinking that, in Kansas at least, I might be ahead of Capote in the plausible manner stakes. I'm not going to turn up on anyone's doorstep, as he did – in the Midwest, in homophobic 1950s America – wearing a full-length fur coat and a boa, and speaking in such a high-pitched voice that many people assumed he was a rather strange-looking woman.

So there's comedy, and a kind of touching bravado, alongside all the other ingredients in the mix: the horrific nature of the crime itself, the drama of detection, and the sheer brilliance of Capote's writing. And it's this distillate of style, destruction and moral ambiguity that has brought me on the road to Garden City. I want to see it for myself, this small city on the high plains which this great, flawed, extrovert, doomed writer had to visit to write his great "non-fiction novel"; to see for myself how close he got – and how close anyone can get – to writing the whole truth. I won't need to stay long. Just long enough, as in Greensburg, beside that tornado-shattered elm, to work out the difference between what I expect and what I find.

The bare facts of the case are contained in eight blue ring-files in the Garden City sheriff's office. Open the first, and there is detective Rich Rohleder's report, banged out on the office Remington: the call at 9:36am on 15 November 1959 to go out to Herb Clutter's farm about half a mile west of Holcomb, a small town six miles outside Garden City. There were four bodies there that looked like they'd been shot, and he had to take the photographs. Turn over a page, and there they are. In the basement, Herb Clutter, 48, the left side of his face blasted away, his right hand tied to his ankles, his pyjamas soaked with blood from the stab-wound in his neck. His son Kenyon, 20, also trussed, lying on a black leather settee, his shot face twisted into a rictus of pain. Upstairs in her bedroom, his sixteen-year-old sister Nancy, her face turned to a dark-stained wall. Finally, her mother Bonnie, lying on her bed, remnants of white adhesive tape on her mouth, her mouth and her skull both wide open.

In the rest of the files, the story unfolds. The statement from Floyd Wells, inmate No. 14323 at Kansas State Penitentiary, about how he'd once told his cellmate Dick Hickock about working for the Clutters, how there was a safe there containing so much money that on payday Herb Clutter could reach in and get $10,000, no problem. How Hickock said that when he was released on parole, he'd drive the 400 miles across Kansas to River Valley Farm, the Clutters' home, with his friend Perry Smith, tie everyone up using Venetian blind cord ("because everyone has Venetian blinds these days"), and torture the old man until he told them how to open the safe. With the money they'd buy a boat in Mexico, maybe use it for drug running. They'd leave no witnesses.

Back in Scotland, I'd phoned up the owner of River Valley Farm, explained who I was, and asked whether it would be alright to drop by. He said it would be fine. I told my son I was going to see the murder house. "Cool," he said.

Now I can quite understand anyone who thinks that this isn't a cool thing to do at all, that it's no more than macabre, book-related ghost-hunting. In this case, I'd agree, which is why I didn't actually take up the invitation. Nearly fifty years on, the house couldn't tell me anything that I didn't already know from looking at the photographs of the Clutter family's murdered bodies over coffee and biscuits in the Garden City sheriff's air-conditioned office. That's more than enough reality for anyone. But because you can't interview the dead, you have to get as close as you can in other ways. Writing this, I think back to two other occasions in the last year when I did get close. In Dublin last November, I sat opposite Christy Brown's brother in the tiny living room of a two-bed-roomed house: the house in which the author of *My Left Foot* grew up, one of a family of thirteen. I asked where the seven-year-old Christy had been sitting on that single, crucial moment of his life when his mother realised that he wasn't the vegetable-brained hopeless case the doctors had described – when, unable to talk, and seemingly illiterate, he picked up a piece of yellow chalk between his toes and wrote the word "Mother". "That'd be just where you're sitting now," Francis Brown told me. A few months before that in Amsterdam, Anne Frank's best friend had shown me the Monopoly set the two of them used to play with after school in the Jewish ghetto. Again, the same frisson of connection.

You can say this is just a very privileged form of literary tourism, and I might agree. But I don't think there's anything wrong with that. If you see what an author saw – above all, if you meet the people an author met – the decades between you and the writer's work can shrink away. You can see, from looking at what remains, what might have been there. You can imagine, for example, what River Valley Farm must have looked like, before it became accompanied in our minds by a dark and menacing soundtrack, or before the photographers started exaggerating its shadows. Ultimately, though, it's just a house. An interesting background, nothing more. In this story of looking for Capote, the people matter far more.

❖　❖　❖

When he wanted to get permission to go to the Clutters' house – or to watch their murderers hang – the man Capote turned to was Clifford Hope. A former Republican state congressman as well as Herb Clutter's lawyer, he still lives with his wife Dolores in the home he grew up in, a hundred-year-old detached clapboard house in a leafy Garden City suburb.

In December 1959, the Hopes and their children were at home. Normally, they would go away for Christmas, to stay with either Dolores's mother or Clifford's parents, but this year her mother had just got out of hospital and couldn't cope with having the grandchildren, and Clifford's parents were visiting his sister out East. So they stayed in Garden City and, knowing there wouldn't be any restaurants open on Christmas Day, invited the two strangers from New York to have Christmas dinner with them. At two in the afternoon, Capote and Harper Lee turned up as promised, with a bottle of Capote's favourite J&B whisky. For the past few weeks, they'd done most of their interviews around Holcomb. Although they'd been staying at a motel in Garden City, they hadn't got to know too many people there. They knew Clifford though: as executor of Herb Clutter's will, he'd given them permission to look around the tidied-up murder scene. Dolores Hope knew Herb Clutter too. She had retired as a journalist on the local evening paper in 1987, but in the early years he'd helped her out on farming stories. Herb was President of the Wheatgrowers' Association in Kansas – an influential job – and they'd go to association dinners, where she also met Bonnie Clutter. "They were just nice people. He was a rigid kind of guy, you know, always in control. But at the same time he was fair. He got things done."

They didn't talk too much about the Clutters that Christmas Day. "Truman had most of the conversation," recalls Clifford. "It was mostly about himself, but it was real interesting. He was a charmer". "And whenever the conversation got to drifting away from him," adds Dolores, "Nelle [Harper Lee] would kind of bring it back. She was like a big sister to him that way, she knew how to keep him happy. She had no airs or graces about her – she was real natural. She'd come across to help me in the kitchen and we'd get to talking, and it was as if I'd always known her." They keep in touch, she adds, showing me a copy of *To Kill A Mockingbird,* which Harper Lee had signed "to Dodie, with love and admiration".

I look around the room one last time. Longingly, because I wish I could have been there. And yet I am. What's the word for when you find yourself in someone else's story? Whatever it is, I'm not finished with it. The next day, Clifford comes along with me to the Clutter farm. He's almost 84 now, and Parkinson's has got a hold of him, so he can only walk in a slow shuffle, and sometimes his sentences briefly dry up in the middle. I don't get impatient, I don't interrupt, because within minutes of meeting him, I've got his measure: he's one of those good-hearted, stoical, commonsensical, Jimmy Stewart type of Americans we've almost forgotten existed. How do I know this? Because when he tells me about visiting Britain during the Second World War, his old eyes light up. At Leominster in Herefordshire he was amazed to read that the English Wars of the Roses were fought more than four and a half centuries before, and to walk to the pub on a road originally built by the Romans. Every town, every village in this part of Kansas was only built after the railway came through in 1872 – but just as I'm starting to think of him as just another American in love with our past, he tells me about how after Dunkirk, British troops had been brought back to stay with people he met at Leominster. "And when they arrived," he said, "they told me they didn't even have any shoes. They were just...." His eyes fill with tears. At that moment I like Clifford Hope enormously. He doesn't belong to the present generation of lachrymose Americans, who feel each other's pain suspiciously easily. He's of that older, greater generation, and I'd guess he doesn't normally give way to emotion. But when he thinks of my countrymen in 1940, of complete strangers, that's his reaction: compassion.

At Holcomb, we bump across the Chicago-Los Angeles main line, and on to the old Clutter farm. We're almost at the geographical centre of the country, and the land is pancake flat and featureless. There's so little rainfall here that a century ago the banks wouldn't loan money to farmers – but now, the Ogallala aquifer feeds sprinklers, each up to half a mile wide, which slowly rotate round enormous fields, giving the landscape, from the air, the look of a yellow-circled pattern blanket. Herb Clutter wouldn't have needed the aquifer's water, as the Arkansas River flows at the back of his farm. Or used to: since they built a dam in Colorado, it runs almost dry. All the orchard trees are long dead too, like half of the Chinese elms that used to line the half-mile drive to his farm. "It's a sad sight," sighs Clifford. On the way, we'd stopped at the cemetery where the Clutters are buried. Nearby are the graves of Alvin Dewey, who led the investigation into their murder – and whom Capote makes the hero of his story – and his wife Marie. Like Capote, Mrs Dewey was originally from New Orleans, and they remained lifelong friends. "I just feel sorry for anyone who never met Truman," she once said. "He was adorable."

Five days after the Hopes' Christmas dinner, the killers were caught. By then, because word had spread about what entertaining company they'd been, Capote and Harper Lee were sought-after party guests in Garden City. Alvin Dewey in particular was a valuable source of inside information for Capote, handing over such things as Nancy Clutter's teenage diary for him to work from. Dewey also allowed Capote to change his words (to make him appear "less like a Sunday school teacher"), and agreed to feature in the book's only made-up scene, right at the end, where he appears at Nancy Clutter's grave. It was a two-way friendship. In return, Capote would ask Hollywood studio executives to show Dewey around on holiday visits, and invite him up to glittering Manhattan social events such as his famed Black and White Ball. He even critiqued Dewey's own attempts at writing. "The thing about Truman is that he could be very mean, but he could also be very kind to his friends," says Clifford later. "Our children have loads of letters he would send them from all over Europe – pictures of his dog, French handkerchiefs, things like that. Course, if you're going to see Duane West, you're going to get a different side altogether."

❖   ❖   ❖

Duane West reaches out to put my right hand in his, his wife Orvileta holds my left, and he says grace at the kitchen table. He asks God to bless the beef potroast we are about to eat, and he prays both for me, his visitor from Scotland, and for his president. At that moment, I can't help warming to him. Because I know that the next day's issue of the *Garden City Telegram* will carry a column by him, calling for Bush's impeachment. I also know that he doesn't really want to talk to me about Truman Capote at all. Why should he? The two men just didn't get on. Writing to the Deweys (he called them "Dearhearts") in 1961, Capote noted, almost boastfully, that he'd got more than halfway through *In Cold Blood* without once mentioning Duane West. This took some doing. West was a 28-year-old county attorney, the chief law enforcement officer in that part of Kansas, prosecuting only his second murder case. For the Clutter murder trial, he'd worked long into the night preparing the briefs; he'd handled the jury selection, made the opening statement, presented over half the witnesses, and cross-examined defence witnesses. Who did more? But you've only got to talk to West for a short while to realise why he and Capote wouldn't have hit it off. A towering, straight-talking hometown Methodist, West doesn't smoke or drink, and has been passionate about politics since childhood. There's little there to appeal to a diminutive, camp, metropolitan socialite like Capote; and the feeling was mutual. To West, character matters, which is why he voted for Gore and Kerry but couldn't bring himself to vote for Clinton.

He's never read *In Cold Blood,* and has no interest in seeing either of the recent films about the case. Why not? Is it really all because of a slighted ego from forty years ago? I think it's more than that. To West, Capote got the case wrong in other ways too. Remember detective Rich Rohleder, the first detective on the murder scene? When he'd finished taking the pictures, and they were bringing the bodies out of River Valley Farm, West asked him who could possibly have done it. "We all thought it was a grudge killing of some sort, but Rohleder said it was probably a robbery and that they were four hundred miles away by now. He was only ten miles out." (The murderers had returned to Hickock's parents' home, 390 miles away in Egerton, Kansas). Alvin Dewey, Capote's hero detective, part of what West calls "the country club set", far from cracking the case, persisted with the notion that the Clutters had been wiped out as part of a vendetta.

Yet look in Capote's book for Rohleder, and you'll find he hardly gets a mention – another example, says West, of someone deliberately written out of the story by Capote. And again, that's odd, because some people claim that Rohleder's photographic evidence might well have cracked the case even if Hickock's former cellmate hadn't fingered him for the murders. But even when that happened, says West, Dewey still refused to believe it, which is why the Kansas Bureau of Investigation didn't send him to the prison to do the interview in the first place. If anyone should be singled out for praise, he adds, it should be the two detectives who then went to Hickock's parents and found that the prisoner's statement checked out. "Know-it-all, know-nothing Duane West", sneers Capote in one of his letters to his hero Alvin Dewey. I'm absolutely not convinced. The man sharing his 76th birthday dinner with a stranger from Scotland, talking about politics, about his home town, and his new career as an artist, entrepreneur and gallery owner, is anything but.

So what is the truth? One truth is that *In Cold Blood* is a work of genius. In structure, approach and writing, Capote tears apart the clichés of crime and punishment. Another truth is that no one story is ever completely told, perfectly free of bias. The one you're reading now isn't either. Every journalist's portrait of events is inevitably skewed towards those who are the most helpful, and so was Capote's.

But look among the footnotes. If Duane West had found out that Alvin Dewey handed over Nancy Clutter's diary to Truman Capote, he could have kicked him off the case. If Clifford and Dolores Hope hadn't invited Capote and Harper Lee round for Christmas Day dinner, they might have carried on being shunned by the important people in Garden City. If either of those things had happened, we might not have *In Cold Blood,* or it might have ended up no better than second-rate. I learnt that much in Garden City: that if you want to go beyond the surface of even a great modern classic, you have to look at the footnotes. Look at Rich Rohleder, typing his first report. At Clifford and Dolores with their two great writer guests on Christmas Day 1959. Maybe even, for a footnote to a footnote, at Duane West sitting on the porch of his house with a visiting Scottish journalist. Because that's the thing about footnotes. Some of them live on after the story's stopped. And if you really want the truth, look between all the footnotes there'll ever be, and you might just find it.

Willy Russell

My first interview in my new job takes me to an elegant Georgian building in Liverpool overlooking the Anglican cathedral and the Mersey beyond. It's September 2000, and playwright Willy Russell — a key figure in my personal populist pantheon — is about to publish his first novel. Years later, my son is revising for an exam on Russell's 'Educating Rita'. One of the questions is the extent to which the play is auto-biographical. "Read this," I tell him.

THE OPENING scene was all wrong. Instead of a Liverpool housewife bustling about in her kitchen making egg and chips for her husband ("Y'know, I like a glass of wine when I'm preparing the cooking. Don't I, Wall?"), there was this tall, deep-voiced man standing at a lectern in the middle of the stage, reading the words he'd written for an actress who was now in hospital with appendicitis. But he read on, about a forty-year-old woman who suddenly realised that she was leading such a little life, whose marriage had collapsed into silences and whose friend had bought her tickets for a holiday on a Greek island but she wasn't sure if she'd dare leave her husband behind, even if it was only for two weeks, what with Joe being the kind of man who shouts at her because she serves him egg with his chips instead of fish. "Wouldn't he, Wall?" And within minutes, every single person in that theatre had forgotten that it was really just a man, delivering words from a stage.

So when the woman, who's called Shirley Valentine, finally goes to Greece, we could all see her there, not the bearded playwright reading in deeply modulated Scouse. And when she told us how she met a Greek called Costas, we could all imagine it, how he reassured her that stretchmarks are marks of life and shouldn't be hidden away and how he bent down to kiss them. And when Shirley turned to the audience and said: "Aren't men full of shit?" we all laughed, relieved that she'd sussed him out: that even when she was living her Greek island dream, she still had more than a toehold on reality.

By then we, the audience, had forgotten about reality altogether. Our disbelief hung suspended, far above our heads. We believed in this woman called Shirley Valentine. And still, the only person on the stage was Willy Russell, the best performer of his own work I've ever heard. The Everyman Theatre, Liverpool, June, 1986. The most magical night of theatre in my life.

There is, Willy Russell tells me, fourteen years later, a real Shirley Valentine. He'd presumed she would have got married and changed her name, but she never did. He still gets the occasional letter from her. She's not a bit like the character in the play and film named after her, but she's just as sparky and bright. Life hasn't ground her down, even though she was in the D form with Russell and all the other sparky, bright thickies in Rainford Secondary. He hasn't changed much since I saw him read, all those years ago. The thick beard has given way to grey designer stubble, and although he had a heart attack last year, you'd never guess. He's 53, but the rangy kind of 53-year-old, who can still wear jeans and a black leather jacket and not look foolish. Even if he hadn't written anything since *Shirley Valentine,* Russell would still be a financially successful writer: his 1983 musical *Blood Brothers* alone would have seen to that. Add on the royalties from *Educating Rita*, all the film deals, and the touring productions all over the world. But now, add to all this his remarkable first novel, *The Wrong Boy*.

The Wrong Boy, like *Shirley Valentine*, is an extended monologue. Its hero, Raymond Marks, is nineteen years old; an alienated teenager and a passionate Morrissey fan. As Raymond travels across northern England to a brain-numbing job in Grimsby, he looks back on a childhood in which nothing seems to have gone right. Expelled from school at the age of eleven by a blinkered headmaster who wilfully misinterprets a simple bit of laddish fun as a sickening outbreak of sexual perversity, he is moved to a new school. Trouble soon follows, because now he has a bad reputation to live up to. His mother, faced by yet further evidence of Raymond's sick mind, and struggling to cope on her own, agrees to send him to a residential school for educationally sub-normal children.

Put like that, it doesn't sound particularly funny. On the page, it bounces between manic highs and gut-wrenching lows. At its core (though not at its outer edges, where coincidences defy even the longest of odds) it's as tightly plotted as a Ruth Rendell. And as Raymond Marks's heroic innocence is progressively undermined by obstructive teachers, obtuse psychiatrists and blame-hunting police, he comes to accept that he is the Wrong Boy, incapable of doing right or of being understood by anyone except Morrissey, the patron saint of bedsit miserabilism.

There must have been times, I suggest, when Russell felt like the Wrong Boy himself. Aged eleven, for example, he was so badly caned for a bit of horseplay that his parents moved him from school. At the next school, the rumour went round both pupils and staff that he'd been expelled, that he was a real hard nut. Sent down to join the original Shirley Valentine in the D form, he left school with a solitary O-level, in English Language, and the casual assumption that he was fit for nothing but a job in the local bottle factory. He agrees that there are some parallels with Raymond Marks in his novel, but insists that he doesn't write autobiographically. Or at least not consciously. "I remember saying to my wife when I was writing *Educating Rita*, 'I don't know where this stuff is coming from, it's got nothing to do with me' and she said, 'What do you mean? Wait till you see it on stage.' And sure enough, six weeks into the run, I'm looking at this glaringly autobiographical play. But the point is that if I'd have been aware of it in the first place I wouldn't have had the necessary liberation to write it." Implicit in *Educating Rita* is the assumption that school fails the overwhelming majority of pupils. "Oh, without a shadow of a doubt. It fails more people than it serves. Even now, in my letters to Shirley Valentine, when we look back on our schooldays, the anger that's still in me comes rushing out. I mean, Shirley's a very bright girl. She shouldn't have been in the D stream. I shouldn't. I could go round that class and there would be fifty per cent who shouldn't."

In *Blood Brothers* there is a scene in which Mrs Lyons, the wife of a factory owner, hovers over a crib containing twins. Their mother, who has six children already, lives in poverty, has just been deserted by their father, and can only afford to raise one of them. She has offered the childless Mrs Lyons the chance to bring up the other. And that crucial moment in which Mrs Lyons makes her choice has echoes, it seems to me, in Willy Russell's own life: one direction, clear as an empty motorway, to opportunity, achievement, contentment, wealth; the other, equally stark, to failure, anonymity, and poverty of expectation. Russell, I imagined, must have reached that crossroads when he was eighteen. He had been a hairdresser for two years, hated it, and wanted to find a course that would allow him to take a bunch of O-levels and the one A-level that would qualify him for teacher training college. At one college, the head told him: "Listen son, you failed at school. You did nothing there, you abused the system. Why should I give you a second chance? Get out!" But there was a second chance. When he went, raging, to the council's education department to complain, he saw, on a pillar by the door, details of just the course he wanted. And another piece of life-changing luck: when he went to the college offering it, there was still a place, provided he had English Language O-level. Which was all he did have.

At that moment, Willy Russell can rejoin the mainstream. He can stop swimming against the tide, can go to teacher training college and learn how to teach drama. In Liverpool's Everyman Theatre in the early 1970s, he will meet John McGrath and Allan Dosser and discover how to uncover the poetry in everyday speech, how to hook into ordinary life in a way that high art can't. And he will write *John, Paul, George, Ringo … and Bert,* be fêted by the West

End at the age of 26, and go on to be one of Britain's most successful playwrights.

Whoa. Stop. That's just one interpretation of Educating Willy. Back to the man himself. He's actually saying something quite different. Could he, I ask, imagine himself without an education? "You mean, would I have gone quietly to me death in a factory? I don't think I would. I'd be like Shirley – the real one. Her spirit is still gloriously intact. But the other thing about a bad education is, it's not all done to us. We conspire in our lack of education, too." And I know where the conversation's turning next. We're looping back thirty-odd years, to an eleven-year-old listening to Radio Luxembourg at night, under the covers in his parents' prefab home. To a twelve-year-old playing Little Richard on his Dansette. To a thirteen-year-old who goes to see The Young Ones at the Liverpool Odeon ten times on the trot ("though I hate Cliff Richard") just to see The Shadows play. To a teenage truant who is learning something more important than the things they teach at school.

Back on Russell's estate, where he lived as an only child (his sister, Dawn, was born when he was seventeen), there was a lad called Tom Evans who was always much better than him when they started learning the guitar. Later on, he was in the group Badfinger. Remember that song "(Can't Live if Living is) Without You"? He co-wrote it. Dead now. Suicide. But in 1961, when they were thirteen, some older kid told them there was only one place to go in town – some cellar in an old fruit warehouse down Matthew Street. "One Sunday night me and Tommy went down to town. We'd to promise our parents we'd be back by 10pm. When we got there we were blown away by the heady scents, the cigarette smoke. There wouldn't be the sweat running down the walls, because this was early on in the evening and there'd be groups on like the Flamingoes or the Fathoms, copies of the Shadows really." His eyes shine at the memory. "To be in a place where you could see a Fender Strat up close ... It was so heady. To hear songs like "Young Blood", "Poison

Ivy", the Chan Romero version of "Hippy Hippy Shake" – all these tunes that you'd heard, but only in your bedroom coming from America. But this was here, in your own town. It was spellbinding.

"We were about to go, because we were worried about getting home, when we saw these guys come on the stage with their hair combed forward, wearing black corduroy – the Beatles. So we had to stay. The first song they played was "Some Other Guy". There was a lot of talk subsequently about how the Stones were a really heavy band, but if you heard the Beatles before they became known for doing Lennon-McCartney – Christ, they were a slab-hard rhythm and blues band. They used to take the hair off your scalp." And that's the way it was, as often as they could get there. There were lunchtime sessions, so they'd skip off school. Sneak past Paddy Delaney, the bouncer on the door, with his tux, cummerbund and diamond studs, down eighteen steps from a dingy backstreet, into a musical paradise. The Cavern.

You didn't need exams for this new music. It was a working-class art form. The people who played it were ordinary young men, from council houses and redbrick terraces, whose mothers were nurses or waitresses and whose fathers were dockers or absent or on the dole. There were three hundred live music venues in the city and, so they always said, a thousand bands. There was a confidence about Liverpool then, even though the city was already starting to wither to what it is today – European City of Culture notwithstanding – all gap sites and Stanley knives and an empty river.

No wonder the teenage Russell would conspire in his lack of education. Once he'd cut his fingers learning chord changes on a cheap steel-stringed guitar, it didn't matter that he was in a dead-end job in a hairdresser's: there were plenty of other ways out, and not just surfing the Merseybeat wave of musical optimism. Hence the green corduroy jacket he bought in his "pretending to be Roger McGough" phase. So he didn't mind too much helping his mother out when her draper's shop was turned over and she'd lost everything because nothing had been insured. He changed it to a hair-dresser's and stayed there for a couple of years until she'd paid back all the debts she'd hidden from his father. When *Educating Rita* came out, the critics all wanted to write about how he'd been a hairdress-er so he must be The Man Who Understands Women. Maybe there's some truth there – but at the time, the music was always vastly more important.

He started off by writing sketches in the back of the shop in the slack times between customers. In the evenings, it would be down to the folk club the Spinners used to run in Brunswick Street, where he would test out his songs, and experience that strange mix of pre-performance anxiety and the ecstasy of hearing laughter just where he'd planned it to be. "I still go on stage terrified" he says. "You've got to keep your performance alive, you've got to fly dan-gerously." Perhaps, at that time, in that place, Willy Russell might have been a success, even with only one O-level. "It's possible. Because what I found in the folk song movement was a whole lot of people who weren't necessarily academic in a university-trained way, but were also very learned and scholarly. Listen to someone like Billy Connolly talk about it. This was an extraordinary group of people, a wonderful seedbed, a great place of learning."

There's a story Willy Russell tells about one of his uncles that isn't actually true, but ought to be. One day his uncle Matt had been persuaded to go to the theatre to see *Waiting for Godot*. He bought the programme and pointed out how stupid it would be to sit through the show. "Look," he said, pointing at the cast list. "There's no mention of Godot here. 'Course he's not going to bloody turn up!" By this, Russell doesn't mean to mock Beckett, but to point out how deep the narrative hook has to be driven into the story for theatre to be truly populist; for it to be as much for people like Rita the hairdresser as it is for Frank, the lecturer. An art theatre *Shirley Valentine*, for example, would be an interior monologue – but intro-duce the Wall as something for her to talk to, and the play instantly becomes wittier and more accessible. In *The Wrong Boy*, Raymond's letters to Morrissey perform a similar function.

Just because Russell's work is so accessible does not, of course, mean it is artless. Listen to the lyrics twist and turn in *Blood Brothers*, follow its compelling chord changes, and you realise that there's more to Russell than narrative drive alone. Listen to him read *The Wrong Boy,* putting all of Raymond Marks's teenage anguish in a pleading Lancashire whine, and you understand how completely he has imagined the character, and how perfectly he has constructed the plot, so that one moment's extended comic riff can slide so smoothly into its darker themes of child abuse and institutional care. He wrote the book, he says, with the aim of producing something that sounded spoken rather than written. He's succeeded. In the voice of this shy, misunderstood teenager, Willy Russell is every bit as convincing, funny and life-enhancing as ever.

P.S. - *Since this interview,* **The Wrong Boy** *has been translated into fifteen languages, and is currently being adapted for television. The paperback is available, published by Black Swan.* **Blood Brothers** *is now in its nineteenth year at the West End. The scripts of* **Shirley Valentine, Educating Rita,** *and* **Blood Brothers** *are all published in paperback by Methuen. At the time of writing, you can check details of touring performances at the "official-unofficial" website, www.willyrussell.com*

Bernard MacLaverty

"What is fiction?" Bernard MacLaverty once asked his English class in Edinburgh back in the 1970s. "It's made -up truth, sir", one girl answered, and he's stuck to that definition ever since. I interviewed him at his home in Glasgow in 2001, when his novel, 'The Anatomy School', was published. It contains more from his own life than any other of his books, as well as taking us deep into the heartland of his fiction: the Belfast of the late 1960s and early 1970s.

HERE IS a scene in Bernard MacLaverty's new novel, *The Anatomy School,* in which the adolescent protagonist, Martin Brennan, is about to lose his virginity to an Australian backpacker in the medical laboratory where he works. Outside, in the night, are the sounds of what may be explosions and probably are, because this is Belfast in the early 1970s. Inside, they are talking about their favourite movies, and he tells the girl he likes Stanley Kubrick's first feature, *The Killing* best, because it chops up time and reassembles it in different, more interesting ways. It's a throwaway remark, but not insignificant. Belfast at that time is *The Killing*: the people doing it are chopping up the past and reassembling it in different ways. But the line also harks back to a more innocent time, earlier in the novel, when Martin was still at school, and had heard about the Kubrick film from a friend much cleverer than him. Maybe he was just pretending to have seen it to impress the girl, the way you do when you're nineteen. A minor detail then; something that flashes between commas and is gone. But MacLaverty's details are the kind that carry weight; the kind you can lean on.

No other novelist has written about the Troubles as sensitively as MacLaverty, who, because of them, left Belfast for Scotland in 1975. In *Lamb* (1980), *Cal* (1983) and 1997's Booker-nominated *Grace Notes*, he has approached, with varying degrees of directness, the emotional consequences of living in the Six Counties after the bombs and shootings became commonplace. In *The Anatomy School*, time is chopped up and reassembled in different, more interesting ways, to cut away under the Belfast we think we know – explosions, banging dustbin lids, terse news bulletins – and reveal a Belfast we don't. A city at peace.

MacLaverty is 58, and his thick thatch of hair is edging from ash grey to white, but he has one of those faces in which you can still see the boy he was. Sitting in his airy, ground-floor flat in Glasgow, he talks of that boy, growing up in a red brick terrace on Atlantic Avenue, north Belfast, wondering why they called an ocean after it. Falling asleep to the sound of Ravel from his father's record player in the sitting room downstairs. Being twelve, and missing him badly when he died of lung cancer. John MacLaverty was a commercial artist on a newspaper. He drew pictures of milk bottles in adverts for dairies, cheery children eating sandwiches in adverts for bakeries, that sort of thing. "I never really got to dislike him because before you're twelve you love your parents. Once the hormones kick in, that all changes, but he died before that happened. I hold him in the highest esteem." He takes me out into the hall. He's just had his sitting-room floor sanded, and a thin layer of wood dust coats the top of the books on the hallway shelves. "Look," he says, blowing the dust off a 1950s child's Bible, illustrated with line drawings. "He did these. They're very simple, but we all thought they were very good."

MacLaverty is rarely more than a sentence or two away from a laugh or a joke, but now he is not. He shuts the Bible carefully, respectfully, and not because he's religious. Then he's off, rummaging into a photograph album of those early days, flicking through his childhood. His uncle, the priest who married his parents. His great-grandparents, stern and scowling into the camera lens outside a Co. Antrim cottage. Himself, playing the tea-chest in his skiffle group, V2, all quiff and grin. His gran at eighteen. "Now she was one of the most timid, peaceful people imaginable," he says. "But she could remember how bad things were back in the 1920s. Once there was a football match and the Protestants were coming down on the tram to support Cliftonville and I remember this, she said someone threw a grenade into the tram of supporters and it hadn't gone off. And it was one of our own who did it, she said." One of our own. Back then, with the Black and Tans taking bloody revenge on nationalist areas, those allegiances meant something. The young MacLaverty knew that: every day, on his way to school at St Malachy's College, he passed the house where, in the early 1920s, the entire MacMahon family had been massacred, except for one child who hid under an upstairs bed. But that was ancient history. Things had changed. The first generation of working-class Catholics to go to university was working its way up. The old tribal divisions were still there, but it was like Rangers and Celtic, nothing to kill or die for. "It comes in waves, you see. In my childhood we were in a trough of peace." That laugh again. At absurdity.

A former teacher, MacLaverty also writes incisively about school from a child's point of view. About the depth of the friendships you make, right at the end, when you're reaching out for all the big questions and don't yet know any of the answers; when conversations can switch, in the space of a breath, from jokes about farting to arguments about atheism. About how you can be revising and the words break apart and swim in front of your eyes. About teachers' nicknames, and the surreal unfunniness of their jokes. You know, when you read MacLaverty, that the details matter.

In *The Anatomy School*, Blaise, a rebellious, atheist boarder at Martin Brennan's Catholic school, decides that the only way to screw the system satisfactorily is by stealing the exam papers. Brennan, the least academic of the gang of three who try to do it – the one most like MacLaverty – knows it's his only hope.

The tension reached in the course of Martin's raid on the cupboard in which the exam papers are kept reaches levels most thriller writers couldn't even begin to match. MacLaverty himself refuses to be drawn on whether he tried anything similar at St Malachy's. "It's like a perfect murder," he laughs. "If you did it, no-one would ever know. And hasn't everyone in their teenage years done something that, had they been caught, would have got them in big trouble?" Either way, Martin Brennan does have a lot in common with his creator as a young man. Both their fathers died, both have passed their exams to the Catholic grammar school, both went on voluntary Church-organised retreats. Both failed all three of their A-levels (including English) and had to stay on another year for the re-sits. Both then went on to work in the medical laboratory of Queen's University. Above all, both lived in a house full of talk. This is the comic heart of the book, and it's worth buying for the dialogue alone. As in an Elmore Leonard novel, you can read it and know instantly which character is speaking, without being told: Martin Brennan's mother, keeping up appearances and ushering the visiting Father Farquharson to the best seat; her friend Nurse Gilliland, who gently torments him with abstruse questions about transubstantiation; "the fair and flawless Mary Lawless", as she calls herself, whose conversational input borders on the bizarre; the patient priest, comfortably relaxed in a house of faith.

Back to Atlantic Avenue. It wasn't quite like the Brennans', but it came close. "I grew up listening to that kind of talk. My father must have been a saint of some sort because he invited my great-aunt Mary, and my grandfather and grandmother to live with us in this Victorian terrace. When you're growing up, you think it's entirely natural, and that everyone else should do this too – have three oldies sharing the house with them. Directly across the street was my father's sister and my other grandfather. My mother would have friends in and as a child you'd listen, sitting in a corner, never dreaming of contributing. Just listening." Just listening is an underrated writerly skill. According to Philip Hobsbaum, the former professor of English at Glasgow University whose informal writers' groups kickstarted literary renaissances in both Belfast and Glasgow, it is the key to MacLaverty's writing. "He has a superb ear," Hobsbaum says. "When I was teaching at Belfast and he'd come along to the group, I remember he was one of the very few with an ear for the harder, more gravelly Protestant voice as well as the Catholic voice he grew up with. He was a lab technician then. I remember him as a quiet, rather shy, man."

Into the rearranged past again. This quiet, shy lab technician would cycle up to Hobsbaum's flat opposite the Catholic chaplaincy of Queen's University, walk past the brooms and mops of the caretakers' department downstairs, and join the other writers in the group. There would be about eighteen of them crowded into Hobsbaum's living room, Seamus Heaney, Paul Muldoon and Michael Longley among them. At school, the scholarship boy who failed all his A-levels never looked remotely in that league. He took from St Malachy's a love of Gerald Manley Hopkins's poetry (which he can still quote at length), and of Shakespeare's *Macbeth*, and a knowledge of science. The last impelled him to a job as a lab technician at the anatomy school, which he took "in the meantime" while he worked out what he really wanted to do. "In the meantime" lasted the next ten years, but it was when his real education began – not just at Hobsbaum's group, but also among his own friends.

MacLaverty is an optimist about learning. He thinks it happens naturally; that people always want to find out more about their world. Well, that's the way it was for him. He learnt more from the five or six friends he hung around with after he'd left school than at school itself. One gave him *The Brothers Karamazov*, which made him want to read more and to see if he could write. Another would make him think seriously about classical music. A third was a philosopher, a fourth a painter. It wasn't precious – this is Belfast, after all, not Bloomsbury – and there was the kind of flyting and slagging that girlfriends would mistake for serious fallings out. "It was a time of learning and excitement in ideas, and interest was always, always underlined by laughter. You'd play poker and it would just be talk, constant talk, constant learning, always probing, always exploring. It was only later on that I realised it was unique. And for that kind of world to be suddenly exploded with hatred and violence was ..." He doesn't finish his sentence. He doesn't need to.

If I were to chop up and rearrange Bernard MacLaverty's life, I would excise the Troubles altogether. Without the distant blasts of bombs as he was writing his finals at Queen's, where he finally went to read English, and without the need to spare his wife and four young children from the effects of daily, nameless fear, he wouldn't be living in Scotland. He wouldn't have written the novels he has, but other ones, just as good. I'd follow, instead, his fictional alter ego's life. The morning after the night that Martin Brennan lost his virginity in *The Anatomy School*, that bright, confident morning when his rites of passage are finally over, he cycles down from the university, smiling to himself. At a bus stop he sees a blonde girl wearing a yellow outfit. A girl he's seen before. A girl he could dream about going out with, but would never dare ask. But now, that morning, full of the joys of life, he does. "That girl by the bus stop, you know," he says with a soft chuckle. "That was Madeleine."

So I'd skip nearly forty years for the last scene. When Madeleine MacLaverty comes into this West End flat, laden with shopping, passes on a message from one of their daughters, and my taxi is waiting and blocking the road and the car behind is honking at it, and so we all make hurried goodbyes and I tell him his book's the best I've read all year and that's where I'd end it. There.

P.S. - *Bernard MacLaverty's novels* **Lamb**, **Cal**, *and* **Grace Notes** *are all available in paperback from Vintage, along with* **The Anatomy School**. *Since this interview, MacLaverty has also published his fifth short story collection,* **Matters of Life and Death**. *He has written and co-directed a short film,* **Bye-Child** *(2003), based on a poem by Seamus Heaney, which was nominated for a BAFTA for Best Short Film, and won a BAFTA Scotland for Best First Director. In 2005, Bernard MacLaverty won the Lord Provost of Glasgow's Award for Literature. His official website can be found at www.bernardmaclaverty.com*

Valerie Martin

I first saw Valerie Martin in London in 2003, when she won the Orange Prize for 'Property' — the only novel on the shortlist I hadn't read. I interviewed her four years later, when she appeared at the Edinburgh Book Festival, where she explained that the core of her new novel 'Trespass' lay in her feelings of anger at repeatedly finding a poacher on her land. Before our discussion widened to explore the symbolic meaning of the poacher, I asked her to describe where she was living at the time.

TO GET to the Martins' old place, you head north from New York up the Hudson valley. After 85 miles, nestled in the gently rolling Catskills, you come across a four-room, eighteenth-century farmhouse with a late-Victorian frontage rather clumsily tacked on. At the back are seven acres of woodland, home to innumerable deer and occasional flocks of wild turkeys. That's where the trouble started. They'd only just moved in, nearly ten years ago, when they heard the gunshots: usually at dawn, but sometimes again at dusk. The poacher was probably just after rabbits, but no matter how often Valerie Martin told herself he was no threat to her, she couldn't stop being annoyed. Maybe he'd shoot her cat by mistake. In any case, it was their land, and already posted with "No hunting" signs. She was planning to clear her woods one day, and build herself a studio to write in. Men prowling around with guns were definitely not part of the picture.

Martin wondered why she was so fixated on catching the poacher. She'd seen him once and tried to warn him off, but he soon returned. The neighbours tracked him down, working out where he parked his car and even where he was from. They considered calling the police. In *Trespass*, Martin becomes Chloe, the fictional protagonist. The usual caveats apply: the parallels are only partial, not entirely deliberate, and certainly not exact. Chloe is a book illustrator, not a writer, but she does work on her drawings in a studio, which just happens to be in the woods at the back of a house rather like the Martins'. Woods where a foreign-looking man roams at dawn and dusk with a cocked rifle.

All this started happening ten years ago, but let's fast-forward five. In 2003, Martin and her husband John, a translator, are among the half-million demonstrators in New York against the Iraq war. Though there isn't a single scene set in that war, it's the entire focus of the novel. Unlike Ian McEwan's *Saturday*, set on the very day of those mass demonstrations on either side of the Atlantic, *Trespass* doesn't debate the morality of the Iraq war: all the characters are steadfastly opposed to it. Instead, and far more subtly and effectively, Martin trains her microscope on the descent into conflict by telling another story altogether, framing the arguments in terms of character rather than politics. "I started writing in 2004, a year after the war began," she says. "That demonstration had been completely under-reported, written up only in the metro section of the papers. It was so discouraging. Everyone felt powerless to stop the big wheel from rolling, and even a year later I felt so frustrated and angry. And I had been thinking about my feelings about the poacher and wondering why I had been so obsessed about that, why I'd felt such real hostility and self-righteousness, why I'd felt so strongly that he had no right to be on my land. Ultimately, it's the difficulty of the liberal consciousness. I didn't want to write about the Iraq war for the same reason I didn't want to write about 9/11 — because what interests me is the tipping point to war, and why my country falls for it over and over again, in Vietnam just as in Iraq right now. So I was searching around for a different war to write about."

For the novel, it needed to be one which produced refugees whose lives might interlace with those of Chloe, her historian husband Brendan, and their only son Toby. At first Martin thought of the Lebanese civil war (she was originally convinced the poacher was

Middle Eastern), before rejecting it in favour of the Croat-Serb conflict of the early 1990s. Her husband knew that there was a strong Croat community of oyster fishermen in the Mississippi Delta; she went down there, and encountered a grizzly giant of a man talking proudly about his student daughter in Dubrovnik while serving them oysters from the back of his pick-up truck. Swap Dubrovnik for New York, and another part of the plot snapped neatly into place.

Salome, the Croat refugee girl, is a student with Toby at New York University, where they are studying international relations. She entrances him, but Chloe, his possessive mother, bitterly resents her, suspicious of her Catholicism, her foreignness, and her hold over him. *Trespass* is exquisitely balanced between a family story and a novel of ideas. Brendan is writing a new history of the Fifth Crusade, also looking at how wars start; trying to uncover the realities of people's lives in the strange country that is the centuries-distant past. As for Chloe herself, she has been commissioned to illustrate a new edition of *Wuthering Heights*. "It was the obvious choice because it is about a foreigner [Heathcliff] who wrecks not just one but two families," says Martin. To Chloe, that was exactly what Salome was doing to her own tight-knit brood.

The novel is driven by character, through shifting, multiple perspectives that Martin uses to show how easily each protagonist might make mistakes about the other. At first, for example, we are shown Salome through Chloe's eyes as a *"cunning little vixen"*. Toby is unsure about his girlfriend's fidelity – an uncertainty which, from his perspective, seems credible. The wider question is, of course, whether Chloe was wrong about the poacher: if she's so wrong about her nearest and dearest, it might only be expected. "I love those ambiguities," says Martin. "Wrong-footing readers is one of the great joys of writing. It's important to make the case for a character: so, for example, you can also read Salome as being brave, smart, and trying to become an American. It's the same with Chloe

— I think she is manipulative and controlling, yet you can also read it as her protecting her son."

Structurally, Chloe's concerns suddenly switch into the background halfway through the novel, as the horrors of war in Croatia, and the story of Salome's mother Jelena, become dominant. Underpinning both narrative strands is a deft study of power relations. The Other — the unnamed poacher, Salome herself — stalks the plot, engendering suspicion, requiring an understanding that is invariably denied. Power relations are a theme of much of Martin's work. *Property* — in which she dissected the hypocrisies and moral corruption inherent in ante-bellum slave-owning society — is perhaps the best example, but it's there too in *Mary Reilly*, her retelling of the Jekyll and Hyde story through the eyes of Jekyll's maid, which was turned into a rather disappointing film starring Julia Roberts.

In *Property*, which beat novels by Zadie Smith and Donna Tartt to win the Orange Prize, Martin admits that she was writing a necessary corrective to one of the stories in her earlier book, *The Great Divorce*. "I'd grown up in Louisiana, where the general line was that the Civil War was about rights of the states rather than slavery itself, that the south was going to reform and there was no need for war, that sort of thing. And although the story [in *The Great Divorce*] wasn't itself about slavery, it was set on a plantation, and when I looked at it later I thought it was a bit romanticised. After I'd written it, I became interested in what slavery was really like, and its impact not just on the slaves but on their owners. I don't think I had thought about what being a slave owner would do to a person who had normal human feelings, so I wanted to write about it more realistically." The honesty of Martin's writing is one of the reasons that Margaret Atwood is such a fan. The two met when Atwood was a visiting professor at Tucsaloosa University in Alabama, where Martin was teaching creative writing, and she was the first person to read Atwood's *The Handmaid's Tale*. "We recognised that we had the same concerns and preoccupations straight away," Martin says, crediting her friend with finding her a publisher after she had been without one for eight years.

Switching effortlessly between the brutalities of the Croatian war and the deep comforts of middle-class American life, *Trespass* shows us, in microcosm, what happens just before we set out on the road to war: how, whether accidentally or through fear and ignorance, we demonise the Other, invent new threats to our society, and panic. Cleanly but unshowily written, there's an engaging clarity about the way she deals with the overcontrolling, overanxious Chloe, convincing you that she may well turn out to be absolutely right to be worried about threats to her land and to her family. Skilfully and without didacticism, in the second half of the story, Martin then points the way to the kind of America that could be at peace with the world, a kind of America we used to see a lot of, but seldom do now.

What, I ask at the end of our interview, happened to the poacher in the woods? "They found out that he was Albanian," she says, "but when they finally cleared the woods at the back of our house, they discovered that he wasn't the only one who had been hunting. They found a platform some deer hunters used to shoot from, high up in the trees."

Martin herself no longer lives there. She's moved on. And so, presumably, has the poacher.

P.S. - *As well as seven previous novels, Valerie Martin has written three collections of short stories, the most recent of which is* **The Unfinished Novel and Other Stories***.*
At the time of writing, **Trespass** *is due out in paperback imminently, and a new novel,* **My Emotions***, is scheduled for publication in the summer of 2009.* **Property***,* **Mary Reilly** *and* **The Great Divorce** *are all available in paperback in the UK.*

A L Kennedy

I've read her books, seen her stand-up comedy act (open-ing line: "I know what you're thinking. Lesbian under-taker"), attended several of her book festival events, watched her chair discussions and give speeches, listened to her on the radio and commissioned reviews from her, but oddly, before November 2007, I'd never interviewed AL Kennedy. We met in a Glasgow café, and she talked about her novel 'Day', which had been published earlier that year.

THROUGHOUT the 1990s, journalists would trudge up the steps to AL Kennedy's Glasgow attic apartment to write about the strange, ascetic-looking, hyper-intelligent young woman who lived there. They'd mention the videos of executions and torture on her shelves, the "blood-red" wallpaper, and her small collection of ceramic eyeballs and prosthetic limbs. Into their note-books, along with this panoply of pain, would go variations on the theme of the tortured artist: insomniac, barely solvent, and in constant emotional distress from either failed relationships or unbearable loneliness. Even then, some things were apparent to any interviewer. The mordantly self-deprecating, self-pitying wit with which she dissected the miserableness of the writer's life. Her hon-esty, her pacifism, her laconic asides. They'd note the dangerous edge to her prose, and her fiction's constant fascination with extreme pain and hurt – and they'd wonder to what extent its roots lay in Kennedy's emotionally troubled childhood in Dundee, and her strained relationship with her father, a psychology professor, after her parents divorced when she was eleven. And although Kennedy frequently used her website to mock their prolific profiles, shooting down even attempts at praise with a barrage of withering put-downs, these portraits of her at least mirrored some of the fic-tion she was writing: dark, bleak, obsessive studies of profoundly dysfunctional relationships that were also shot through with a lacerating, cold-eyed intelligence. Her book *On Bullfighting* (1999), an autobiographical journey driven by queasy obsessions, spelled out her mental anguish even more clearly. In it she wrote how, wracked by pain in her neck, grieving for her beloved maternal grandfather, and having lost the will to write, she climbed out of the window of her fourth-floor flat and was about to jump to her death. At that moment, she heard someone in a nearby flat singing "Mhairi's Wedding" ("step we gaily, on we go"). Distracted, she chose life.

All this I knew already. I also knew that I'd been avoiding interviewing her. Why? Fear of being impaled on her website's wall of shame? Perhaps, but only partly. There were reasons why I couldn't have interviewed her for two of her books – conflicts of interest, mainly – but those are pettifogging excuses, not answers. I admired her criticism, laughed at her stand-up comedy routine, didn't argue back when friends told me they thought she was one of the best writers in these islands. But respect isn't the same as like. AL Kennedy seemed too aloof for 'like'; her fiction too crisply intelligent, too uncompromising, for the kinds of qualities we might find 'likeable' in fiction: occasional hope, the possibility of happiness, a certain tenderness with minor characters.

And then I read her novel *Day* and changed my mind. I'd got AL Kennedy wrong. Maybe some of those profile-writers had too: perhaps I'd just been misled by their insistence on her intimidatory genius, her enigmatic bleakness, and so on. Perhaps what I'd read about her wasn't the whole truth. *Day*, though still filled with pain and loss, is on a much vaster canvas than anything she has written before: the firebombing of Hamburg, the London Blitz, the beginnings of genocide, a murder on the home front, a forced march from a prisoner of war camp, a love affair. Other writers can and have done this, although few with that depth of interiority which allows us to see the wartime world as clear as, well, her protagonist, Alfred Day. And there's something else, something I hadn't expected from a pacifist: a portrait of war that has room for its camaraderie as well as its tragedies, its mad laughter as well as its numbing grief.

Kennedy has learned something from those 1990s interviews – so, in the week that *Day* was shortlisted for the Costa Book Awards I met her, not in her flat, but in a Glasgow tearoom. She tells me she had been fascinated by the Second World War for years, but the first inspiration for the novel's complex, time-slipping narrative came when she read a magazine article about an ex-PoW who went back to Germany in 1949, to a film set which recreated Stalag Luft III, to be an extra in *The Wooden Horse*. The notion of a former prisoner returning in order to relive his past as fiction intrigued her. That was what she decided Alfred Day would do too, but what kind of man was he? "I liked the idea of him being a tail-gunner. He sees everything backwards. It's the part on the Lancaster in which the highest percentage of guys were killed, and he's cut off from the rest of the crew in his turret." For three years – when she was also finishing off *Indelible Acts*, her latest collection of short stories, and writing her last novel, *Paradise* – she found out more about him. Research took away some of the blank page's tyranny, but it also made practical sense: "Otherwise you just start and don't know where you are going and have to rewrite endlessly. I spent a huge amount of time on the nature of wartime gunnery. It's not that you're actually going to use any of it, but although the characters are invented, everything to do with the context has to be factual. It's as though you're paying attention on behalf of someone else."

She tells me about going to the armoury of the Imperial War Museum and holding a Browning .303 machine gun in her hands, breathing on it, trying to warm it, because that's the way it would have been for Alfred Day. The barrels of all four of the guns would have grown hot as he swivelled them around in the turret at the tail of the Lancaster, fired off a few blasts, sometimes wondering what the point was, as bullets pinged off the other planes' fuselages.

The image is fixed in my mind: this Quaker-influenced pacifist, bending down to smell the Browning's slightly warmed metal, reading the Lancaster gunners' training manual, learning about targeting trajectories and aircraft silhouette recognition and flak and firestorms. For the three years she was writing the book, she says, she only read fiction from the 1940s. So much research: I'd never expected that. "You have to research in depth, because otherwise you wouldn't have enough confidence, or I wouldn't, anyway. You have to know how you would be, what colour the linoleum was, what the soap was like, what the tea tasted like and what brand of cigarettes you smoked. If you do the research slowly, organically, it remains a living thing and stays with you. So part of me now is forever in seventeenth-century France [after the research for *So I am Glad*] and part of me will forever live between 1940 and 1949. It's kind of weird." She didn't actually go up in a Lancaster herself, because you can't. There's only one Lancaster bomber in Britain that still takes to the skies, but no longer with civilians on board. After she'd finished her research and was writing the book, though, Kennedy did at least get the chance to clamber on board another Lancaster, earth-bound but with its four Merlin engines firing, as if ready for take-off. "It's a lovely machine," she says. "Not that I'm a fan of machines, but I wanted to check out what it felt like on the runway, all engines going. It was amazing – although if you're under it, maybe not so amazing." An aside which, in turn, leads to another reason for writing the novel. "I've been interested in mass bombing on civilian populations for years, even before we started subdividing stones into gravel and sand in Afghanistan and then the pre-war and war bombing of Iraq."

For all her background knowledge, historical analysis and the obvious contemporary parallels, Kennedy doesn't press Alfred Day and the rest of his Lancaster crew into the service of any didactic message. Day's ways are not hers: he doesn't moralise about the destruction his crew is wreaking on the ground below them; he himself is violent, damaged, vengeful, even as he looks for love to heal him. I tell Kennedy that if I had a criticism of *Day*, it would be that sacrificial patriotism – of the kind that was abundant in 1940 when this country's very existence was at stake – is never shown as any kind of motivation. "But when you read people's diaries," she counters, "the number of people who were parroting the government line was ... nil, actually! People were a lot more canny and complicated than that. In any case, he was joining up in 1942-3, past the point where he might have felt like that." It's not just the war that interests Kennedy but the way in which, for someone like her – born in 1965 – it has gradually been replaced in the nation's consciousness by books and films about it. Along with that comes a certain amount of mythologising, as the stark pain, danger and horror of war start to fade. Indeed Alfred Day, in his walk-on role in the PoW film, is himself part of the process.

The scenes on the film set nudge Kennedy's novel towards the surrealistic absurdities of anti-war novels like *Catch-22*, but never so far that you forget the heart-in-mouth terrors of the war itself. She describes the experience of flying into a wall of flak, and the few peaceful, almost incorporeal moments when the engine is still after a successful mission, and Day's own fall into the agonising tendernesses of love, with equal perfection. It feels right. It feels felt. It doesn't feel researched. Along with the realism of war, Kennedy shows some of its finer emotions too, like the way the Lancaster's genial skipper promises Day that he'll fly him on his final mission, when he would otherwise be with a crew of strangers. Or the way the amiable navigator respects Day's willingness to educate himself, and helps him out. And, over all, the quality of the human bond between six men who know that all their lives depend on each other, who develop wry rituals for survival; always leaving something unfinished, some fears unspoken.

In a plot that's packed tight as a parachute, the chronology is bent back on itself, yet ultimately unfolds with a silky smoothness.

And as they take off for their last mission, you can't help caring deeply about all six of her crew. Kennedy wrote the last seventy pages over three days, in a rush of Red Bull-fuelled energy. "It was very emotionally draining, because so many of them die. At the end, when Alfred is in the PoW film set, he's not sleeping either, just remembering them. They all get to you. Well, they did to me anyway."

On a book tour in Germany a couple of months ago ("such a civilised country; now it's us who are fighting pre-emptive wars and having people tried for torture"), that's the part she chose to read out, when Alfred Day is singing "Jerusalem" to a last concert party in the fake PoW camp. When she finished, there was a short silence, then enormous, grief-stricken applause. Kennedy, who is awesomely modest, says that was nothing to do with her. I pick her up on the phrase, because it sounds phoney: a kind of Calvinist modesty, pushed to extremes. "It's really nothing to do with me," was what, back in 1991, a 25-year-old Kennedy mumbled into the microphone while accepting her first literary award in Scotland. Of course it is everything to do with her. But no, she says of that night in Germany. It was just the moment. Just the weight of history on her audience and some of it lifting. Just because we're human.

Nothing to do with her? You be the judge. This is what she read about Alfred Day, in his last day on the film set, belting out "Jerusalem", the way all his crew used to do when marching out to the waiting Lancaster; willing them back to life:

"And he can believe that if he opens his eyes the benches will be full of all the boys lost to the sky and his friends the closest, his crew the closest, so near that he can take their hands and know that they are well and never were harmed and never were frightened, never lost.

And he can believe that he is forgiven.

He can believe so much, the truth of it makes him weep."

P.S. - *Since this interview, **Day** won the 2007 Costa Book of the Year Award.
All of A L Kennedy's fiction is published in paperback by Vintage; **On Bullfighting**
is published by Yellow Jersey Press. Her official website is at www.a-l-kennedy.co.uk.
At the time of writing, the website lists Kennedy's forthcoming appearances as a
stand-up comic.*

Looking For Anne Frank

In her diary, Anne Frank described Jacqueline van Maarsen as her best friend. After I read her revealing 2007 memoir of that friendship I visited Amsterdam and asked Jacqueline and her husband Ruud (who also had a secret childhood in hiding from the Nazis) to take me round the city they would have known in their terrifying teenage years. It's hard to imagine the complete antithesis to the cosmopolitan, ultra-civilised place Amsterdam is today, but the van Maarsens showed me where to look...

JACQUELINE van Maarsen, brings the board game she used to play with Anne Frank into the living room of her elegant Amsterdam flat. "Look," she says "almost as good as new." There's a crack down the middle of the 1938 Monopoly board, but all of the streets' colours are exactly the same as those we play on today. The streets themselves are from all the cities in the Netherlands: Amsterdam, where the two twelve-year-olds rolled the dice against each other, is dark blue; the most valuable. The miniature houses are the same shade of green, the hotels an identical red. The counters are different, but not much: cardboard images of a racing car, a battleship and so on, stuck on to a wooden base. The jail image hasn't changed either. You take cards from two stacks: *Allgemein fonds* (Community Chest). And *Kanz.* Chance.

It was 1941 when Anne Frank and the girl she wrote of as her best friend were playing Monopoly in van Maarsen's parents' flat in Hunzestraat, and there wasn't much chance to go round for people like them. Of the four hundred people at the Jewish school where they met that year (state schools being suddenly shut to yellow star-wearers), only half survived. Those kinds of chances have statistics behind them that the human heart cannot handle. Here are some. Watch them slip glassily past: 1,500,000 murdered children; 104,000 murdered Dutch Jews; 93 trainloads of 1,000 people running east from the Netherlands to the death camps, places like

Auschwitz-Birkenau, which took up 25 square miles of this earth.

Perhaps, if you're like me, and lost no relative to the trains and to the camps, those numbers might have as little meaning as the numbers on the Monopoly money on the middle of the board. There's a book that might help here, and van Maarsen hands it to me. It's three inches thick, 720 pages, as dense with type as a phone directory. She's marked it up so that its pages open at entries for friends and family. There are far too many of them: even if you only count close family, her husband Ruud has 73 relatives in it. Normally, she says, she can't bear to open it; it's just too upsetting. Here, in that book of the Dutch Jewish Holocaust dead, is just one of the entries.

**FRANK, Anne: Born Frankfurt am Main, 12.6.1929.
Died 31.3.1945, Bergen-Belsen.**

There's page after page of Franks alone.

If Anne Frank wrote one of the first books about being Jewish in the Holocaust, then Jacqueline van Maarsen's might well be among the last. That's what brings me to the door of her home on Beethovenstraat. That, and the long-dead teenager who played the Monopoly game with her all those years ago in Hunzestraat, just half a mile north towards the city centre. Anne Frank's story was always the one that stayed in the mind, even when those Holocaust statistics slid away. After the war, the Dutch uncovered two hundred other diaries written by Jewish children in hiding, but it's hers that still speaks the clearest. There's war in the background, of course; and on a tiny map on the wall of the secret annex over the spice warehouse on 263 Prinsengracht, where the Franks lived in hiding for two years, its course is charted. But there's still chance. The Allied armies are closing in, moving north towards the Belgian border. And for a while, it's as if we can slow down time and imagine mending its mid-century horrors.

For two years, this is a small quarantine ward in Hitler's Europe, where good still stands every chance of triumphing in the outside world: the overwhelming good symbolised by the actions of the Franks' four Dutch helpers, and therefore part of the everyday life of the eight Jews they are protecting. There's goodness in the lanky accountant van Kleeman, bounding up the stairs to cheer them up, never a word of his own worries, even though the stress is giving him stomach ulcers. There's goodness in Victor Kugler, the Lutheran who brings Anne cinema magazines every Monday, so she can cut out the pictures and paste them on her wall. It's the same with the secretaries: Bep (Elisabeth Voskuljl), Anne's friend and confidante, and the redoubtable Miep Gies, who is still alive, now in north Holland with her son. And maybe our minds can't take in the Holocaust, but this is different.

Miep, God bless her, was even looking after a conscientious objector, whom she never mentioned to anyone. Eight forged ration cards for eight people who shouldn't exist: daily food for eight people, and never mind a damn what lies she had to tell in the shops. The secret annex is a tiny world, but it still has its dreams. "In spite of everything," writes Anne, "I still believe people are really good at heart." That's how Hollywood ended its 1959 film based on the diary, not with her actual death in Bergen-Belsen, and it's easy to see why. We, all of us, can only take so much reality: much better the reality of the secret annex years, when those in hiding are still connected to the world, with the Westerkerk clock across the road still chiming through the quarter hours, the chestnut tree still growing, and, on good nights, British planes flying east towards the Ruhr under a bombers' moon. Better any of that than what came after.

Because Stalin was right: "A single death is a tragedy, a million deaths is a statistic." That's why the Anne Frank House gets its million visitors a year: because genocide defeats our imagination in a way mere tragedy doesn't. But is it really impossible to understand a million deaths without them becoming a statistic? Perhaps the way to change the focus is to look at the story of Jacqueline van Maarsen, the girl who lived.

Jacqueline and Ruud are bright, companionable, clearly devoted to each other and, although they're in their late seventies, they can't do enough for me. I want them to show me the Amsterdam of 1941, so they usher me into their Renault Megane and we set off in search of lost time. Hunzestraat first. By the time Jacqueline and her family got there, in September 1940, they were going down in the world. Three moves in four years (I can't get that Monopoly image out of my head), each time a flat smaller than the one before. The Nazis invaded in March that year, and already Jacqueline's parents had sold their antiques, their paintings and the best of their furniture. Her father, a Jew, had already seen his business go bust; her mother, a French dressmaker, born a Catholic, was about to see hers go the same way. Miep lived almost opposite. Later, Jacqueline would see her scurrying off in the mornings, apparently to work, but actually to the shops to work her secret daily miracle. Ruud had been born just around the corner, in Lekstraat, though he only lived there until he was five. By this time – 1943 – he was himself in hiding, with the family of a poorly paid but devoutly Christian council official in the east of the country. "At first I went with my mother," he tells me, "but after a couple of days we were told we had to be separated. That's what mostly happened, which is why the Anne Frank case is so exceptional. I'd been there about three days in this simple house with its thin walls when one night I overheard the grandmother saying to the daughter 'How can you take such a child into your home? I can't believe you're doing it – you're just endangering your children and your family.' I was thirteen, and I thought that would be the end for me." It wasn't. He stayed with the family for another two years, taking a correspondence course under a false name. No-one challenged the family's claim that he was a sickly nephew from the city. His mother managed to pass herself off as a maid in another city. Only his father, an asthma sufferer, was looked after – badly – by people who did it for money, rather than out of human decency.

It was from Hunzestraat that, one day in 1942, Jacqueline's mother set out to Euterpe Street, to beg the SS for reclassification as a non-Jew. The biggest chance card of them all. It worked. Instead of being sent immediately to jail – or worse – she and her two daughters were allowed to survive. Even more chancily, her husband bribed a doctor to say that he'd been sterilised. That worked too. You can't find Euterpe Street on the map now: tainted by its association with the Nazi-commandeered school at which Mrs van Maarsen pleaded with bureaucrats for her family's lives, it's been renamed after Gerrit van der Veen, a Resistance hero who in 1943 fire-bombed the Registry Office containing records of Amsterdam's 70,000 Jews. The card index caught fire, but by then most of the Jews had already been deported. Rounded up in raids across the city, they'd been taken by tram – the No 8 service, now also shamed out of existence – to the theatre near to the Jewish school that was the first stop en route to the death camps.

So it passes by the Megane's windscreen, the Amsterdam of 1941. Nothing remains of the ghetto, already empty of inhabitants when it was stripped for wood in the deadly cold winter of 1944. But there, on Beethovenstraat, is the café where informers used to eavesdrop on Jews; on Willemsparkweg, the grocer's where a boy who grew up to be a Dutch Nazi bullied Jacqueline into stealing plums. We drive on to the Jewish school, now a further education college specialising in courses on cosmetics, where Anne and Jacqueline first met. Finally, to Merwedeplein, where the Franks lived before they were forced out into the secret annex, in a house that still has no plaque outside it. "They say they're afraid it would get vandalised by neo-Nazis," says Jacqueline, in a tone that says she doesn't really believe it. And as we drive past canal-side cafés where tourists take a break from sightseeing in one of Europe's most beautiful capitals, I really do get a sense of that hidden, Nazi-occupied Amsterdam. It starts to join up in my mind, and it takes me by surprise, because it's not what I expected at all.

It's a modern place, this Amsterdam of 1941. I feel at home in it. The Merwedeplein flats were only two years old when the Frank family moved there in 1934. The twelve-storey tower block behind it, then the highest in the whole city, the one Anne and Jacqueline called "the skyscraper", belongs in my world as solidly as if it had been built in the 1980s. The bookshop round the corner from where Anne lived is still in business. Nearby streets have been gently yuppified with trendy bars and sought-after delicatessens. Apart from the parked cars, Hunzestraat has hardly changed either. Perhaps because we want to distance ourselves from anything as primitive as genocide, we forget that round-ups of Jews took place in modern streets just like the ones we live in. From the Anne Frank House, you don't really get that sense of the Holocaust as something happening in a contemporary urban setting, but you do if you're driven round 1941 Amsterdam by the van Maarsens. The synagogue just round the corner from Hunzestraat, for example, only opened its door in 1938. The flats and houses from which Jews were dragged in *razzias* (raids) could easily be the ones we pass by on our way to work. These are all modern buildings in a thoroughly modern cityscape. It's disconcerting.

I end up in Hunzestraat because, for Jacqueline, it has the strings of three fates tied to it. The great-hearted Miep, among the best of gentiles, going off to feed the Jews across town in the secret annex. Jacqueline's mother setting out to face the Nazis and save her family. There's a ghost of a link with her husband Ruud, born just around the corner near that new synagogue. And there's another ghost too, because it's to Hunzestraat that Otto Frank finally calls one day in 1945. He wants to talk to Jacqueline about his Anne. In his hands, he's got her diary, and as he reads it, he is starting to discover the daughter he never realised he had. One day soon, he says, he's going to publish it.

P.S. - *My Name is Anne, She Said:* **Anne Frank** *by Jacqueline van Maarsen is published by Arcadia Books.*

Robin Jenkins

In 2002, three years before he died, I met Robin Jenkins in his plain farmhouse overlooking the Clyde near Dunoon. He was 89, and had already written twenty-five novels, the best of which had earned him a reputation as "Scotland's Thomas Hardy", the country's finest novelist since the Second World War, in which he planted a quarter of a million trees instead of fighting. He was a reluctant interviewee, unwilling to talk about his background or influences. Oddly, that didn't seem to matter at all.

W E BEGIN with a ghost: an image of a man in a big khaki coat; a soldier home on leave from Flanders. That's almost all Robin Jenkins can remember about his father. He died in 1920, when his son was eight. It was the war that finished him, he says. I am sitting in Jenkins's kitchen, 82 years later. To my left, the view. There used to be buzzards out there, resting on the post above the farmhouse. They've gone now, so the chaffinches have returned to the beech trees by the corner of the fields. He keeps binoculars in two rooms to watch them, just as attentively as he watches the nuclear submarines slinking back up the grey-green Clyde, half a mile away.

That the shadow of war has marked all of Jenkins's life might not be immediately apparent. In all the novels he wrote over the previous half-century it rarely emerged as a subject in its own right. Stinging satires on the trivial dreams of Lowland Scotland, sharp comedies of small-town manners, insightful studies of the hypocrisies of Scots on the make: for all these themes, there is no better living writer. To Douglas Gifford, Professor of Scottish Studies at Glasgow University, Jenkins is Scotland's Thomas Hardy. He goes even further: without Jenkins closing off the retreat into the myths of a romanticised past, he says, there'd be no James Kelman and no Irvine Welsh. Jenkins himself doesn't agree. Thrawn about what he doesn't go along with and reticent about what he does, he is reluctant to talk about himself and, to some extent, his books. So there are occasional pools of silence between us in that kitchen, as we both look out at the view south towards the Cumbraes, because that seems to be Robin Jenkins's way of dealing with questions he doesn't much like. There's no offensive edge to those silences; they seem natural, unforced. Sometimes even eloquent.

Here is a list of the subjects on which the silence falls. His childhood. Poverty. His teenage years. Why he became a conscientious objector in the Second World War. How it affected his writing. Whether he feels alienated by Scotland today, and what parts of it he would be unable to write about. Some of the answers, he says, are in the novels. Here's a possible example from his latest, the bleakly comic *Childish Things*, in which the septuagenarian protagonist, Gregor McLeod, describes how he has always hidden the truth about his poor childhood: "*They did not know, no-one did, that from the age of eight, when my father had died, I fought myself into the habit of never showing how unhappy I felt, how uncertain, how close to despair. I had kept it up all my life.*"

Later, when Gregor is asked to become an American film star's biographer, he advises her against being totally honest about her past: "*You don't have to reveal things just because they're true. You're entitled to keep them to yourself.*" I quote it back at Jenkins. He smiles. It's an answer of sorts. "I've never talked about my background or the influences on me," he says. "I've never thought carefully about why I have this attitude about wanting to keep these things to myself. I think most writers are like me in that. A book is ninety per cent subconscious. It comes out of you. Often I don't understand why I do or say certain things."

But being a conscientious objector in the Second World War must surely have been different? "I refuse to accept that there's such a thing as a just war," he says. His anti-war stance is consistent across the decades, and the nuclear submarines prowling around the

Firth of Clyde — the issue at the centre of his 1978 novel *A Would-Be Saint* — seem only to have hardened his position. "I see no reason to be hopeful that the human race won't wipe itself out with these weapons, maybe not next year, maybe not even in the next fifty years, but sometime in the future that will happen. Or at least it will unless more people take up the 'wrong-headed' position I did."

Where did those principles begin? He offers some clues. His father was, he says "a machine-gunner, by God", and although he refuses to discuss his childhood, it is plain that his mother had a hard time after his death. His much-missed wife May also lost her father to war at an early age. "But I never heard her saying anything bitter about what happened. In fact, I don't think she ever discussed him with me." What did May think of him being a conscientious objector? "May kept things to herself, even from me. I don't know what her attitude was to it. She never discussed it. But her own father was killed when she was three, so if anyone was going to have sympathy with my views it should have been her. Her own mother was a fairly formidable woman and I always regarded her as fairly right-wing. But never once did she make a single criticism of me. I suddenly realised: why should she? She had a hard time of it, going out as a cleaning lady and so forth to bring up her family. Her grateful country allowed her to do that. No, people were fairer to us than you might have thought."

Jenkins spent the war years working for the Forestry Commission. "I reckon I must have planted 250,000 trees in Argyll. All around west Loch Tarbert. Evergreens, always. Sitka and Norway spruce, Douglas fir. I remember going back there and seeing the trees I planted towering above me." He still likes trees, and brought up his children to be able to tell the difference between them. As in his 1955 novel *The Cone Gatherers*, a modern classic with a regular place on the Scottish school curriculum, trees are the force of life. In the novel, the two brothers who are the seed-gatherers of the title are posted on an estate under the supervision of a gamekeeper, whose life is deformed by hate. The conflict between them is essentially that between goodness and violence in human nature – the very conflict that turned Jenkins into a conscientious objector in the first place.

The preoccupation with moral choice dominates Jenkins's fiction more than that of any other modern Scottish author, according to Professor Gifford. What this means in his books is that descriptions are spare and sparingly used: the moral dilemma is at the heart of Jenkins's writing, not the floweriness of the prose. When he was a teacher at Dunoon Grammar School, to which he returned in 1967 after a decade working abroad in Afghanistan, Spain and Borneo, he applied the same principle to his teaching, marking out whole pages of Sir Walter Scott which his pupils could ignore, so as to get to the bones of the plot. Even as a reader, he skips descriptions whenever he comes across them. Bit of a puritan then? Perhaps. When he was working for the British Council in Barcelona, a city May loved, he quit the job because it didn't allow him enough time to write. She died twelve years ago. A twinge of pain one Tuesday afternoon, as they were about to go to the supermarket, and she was dead by nightfall. They had three children: two daughters and one son. Colin died, also of a heart attack, aged 42. Four days ago his daughter Anne, who lives in Virginia, went into hospital for an operation. She'd had two heart attacks already.

Anne used to live in San Diego, and he and May would go over and stay with her for months at a time. He liked the city, even thought of living there. Would have done too, if it hadn't been for the health insurance. It's hard to imagine. He's just too Scottish, too much his own man, too much of a rebel. In *Childish Things*, Gregor McLeod, visiting his daughter in San Diego, deliberately takes the bus. There, and in the public library, he meets the hidden poor of a rich city – just briefly, admittedly, but for long enough to realise that he would be uncomfortable in a society with such rigid divides between the haves and the have-nots. What can Scotland offer instead? He wonders sometimes, now that his legs are too weak for golf or much walking. Sometimes he forgets, and starts thinking about, say, going to Port Appin for a week or two. Change of scenery. Do him good. "Then I suddenly think: dammit, I'd be as alone there as I am here. No, it'd just be a waste of time."

Another pool of silence. If he were self-pitying, there'd be a breaking voice, a watering eye. There is neither. "The thing I'd miss most isn't the landscape. It's the people. I might not seem very interested in the people I meet, but I am."

"But you don't like talking about yourself?"

"No, that's true."

I look across the kitchen table. Scotland's finest living novelist is gazing out of the window. In the garden below, outside the front door which May always wanted him to use for visitors, but which he still never does, a slight breeze runs through the hydrangeas and rhododendrons. Beyond them it riffles through a fine stand of elms and blows through the new yellow-green leaves of the beeches, planted by someone else, back in a braver, starker, more emotionally reticent age.

P.S. - *Childish Things* is available in paperback from Canongate, who also publish *The Cone-Gatherers*, *Poor Angus*, *The Changeling* and *Just Duffy*. Of Robin Jenkins's other novels, *The Thistle and the Grail*, *The Missionaries*, *Love is a Fervent Fire*, *The Sardana Dancers*, *A Very Scotch Affair*, *Some Kind of Grace* and *Matthew and Sheila* are all available in paperback from Polygon.

Ian McEwan

The London restaurant in which we had arranged to meet was closed because of a gas leak, so he invited me round to his house in Fitzrovia for soup and sandwiches. He was politely affable, yet so precise in his language that sometimes silences formed while he searched for the right word. He was generous with his time, and over the next two hours talked me through the genesis of his 2007 novel 'On Chesil Beach.'

IT BEGAN, as not much else does, in Knoydart. Not as an idea for the story, or the first inklings of character, or an opening scene ready-formed. But Ian McEwan had been on holiday on the Highland peninsula usually known as "Britain's last wilderness" for the last two summers, fishing in lochs where he never saw anyone else, walking on empty hills. That first summer holiday, he opened his notebook and jotted down a few adjectives: *Forgiving. Wry. All-knowing.* Whatever his next story would be, that was the way he wanted to tell it.

Back in England, a few practice paragraphs and a first sentence: *"They were young, educated, and both virgins on this their wedding night and they lived in a time when conversation about sexual difficulties was plainly impossible."* Straight away, he slides into the present tense, the way only a forgiving, wry, omniscient narrator can, before slipping back to the past; to 1962 and the smoothly unfolding story of his new novella, *On Chesil Beach*. Edward and Florence are both 22, just married, and now about to spend their first night together. It is a disaster. Edward's impatience, Florence's unspoken fear of sex — all unpicked in McEwan's trademark controlled, concise prose — will see to that. The love between them is absolutely credible, but so too are the silences, anxieties and misunderstandings that will drown it. This is a hauntingly wistful study of life's lost chances, written with the sustained intensity of a born short story writer, yet fleshed out with a great novelist's sense of anteriority and interiority.

From a writer of McEwan's stature, one expects nothing less. No living author is more central to British literary culture. His 2002 novel *Atonement* sold more than a million copies in the UK alone; the one before it, *Amsterdam*, won the Booker Prize, and the one after it, *Saturday*, won the James Tait Black Memorial Prize in 2006. Right now, he's finishing an opera libretto and working as executive producer on the "very promising" film adaptation of *Atonement*. We're in his house in Fitzrovia, London; the one in which Henry Perowne, the protagonist of *Saturday*, wakes up before dawn at the start of the novel, and looks down contentedly at *"the perfect square laid out by Robert Adam enclosing a perfect circle of garden – an eighteenth-century dream bathed and encircled by modernity"* before looking up to see a plane on fire and losing altitude. McEwan's publicist has assured me that this is the last of only three interviews he'll be giving to the British press for *On Chesil Beach*. Sitting opposite him in his living room, I try to imagine being Ian McEwan. There's a copy of *Scottish Field* on the coffee table between us and a triptych of Peter Howson drawings on the walls behind, so I start there, with Scotland. With Knoydart, and those deserted lochs. With Dumfries and Galloway, where he's thinking about staying when he comes up to Edinburgh for the Book Festival. With Harris, where he and his wife, Annalena, went on a walking and writing holiday in January, the first time he had been on a Hebridean island. With Glasgow, where Annalena was born and many of her family still live, and where his son is researching AIDS symptoms in cats and lions for his Ph.D. Glasgow is where his father, a career soldier for nearly five decades, came from: the barracks he was first stationed in are just a hundred yards from where McEwan's son now lives. Some day, he says, he'll probably write about his father. Not a linear memoir, because the predictability would bore him, just as first-person narration does in fiction. Too easy, too obvious; too much, presumably, like lochs where everyone else fishes.

That's the reason, too, that he doesn't want to discuss the stranger-than-fiction story that appeared in newspapers earlier this year, about the discovery of his long-lost elder brother, a 64-year-old bricklayer called David Sharp. "It was as much a surprise to my half-brother and half-sister as it was to me when he got in touch," says McEwan, "but that was five years ago. The fact of my new brother was never a secret. I told loads of people, but I didn't talk to the press, and they think a thing is a secret if they're not told about it. It's just like Thomas Pynchon: he hates being called a recluse. He just doesn't talk to the press, but that's hardly the same thing."

McEwan's mother, who was born near Aldershot, left school at fourteen to work as a chambermaid. "She was a rather timid person, but agonisingly sensitive," he says. "The novelist in me is certainly down to her." In an essay, he has written about how "her peculiar, timorous relationship with language" – especially when dealing with "posh people" – shaped his own writing. In his first short stories, his prose was similarly wary; a precise kind of uncertainty, immaculately honed. People praised him then, as now, for that hard, unshowy style, always poised no matter what grotesqueries he might be writing about: feral children in *The Cement Garden*, sadomasochistic intrigue in *The Comfort of Strangers*. His first collection of short stories, *First Love, Last Rites*, had the lot: lonely sadists, incest, castration and paedophilia, all wrapped up in prose as cool and sharp as a Sabatier knife.

These days, McEwan admits that he might have been trying too hard. "Back then I used to go around saying I didn't write to shock people. Now I've come round to thinking that's exactly what I was trying to do." His more recent novels, however, have been so compellingly character-driven as to bury the old "Ian Macabre" tag almost out of sight, and *On Chesil Beach* is no exception. "It didn't feel like a historical novel, but it is definitely from another time. I was drawn to these two characters who would have experienced both sides of the 1960s, from the beginning of the decade, which actually had more in common with 1935, when the first half of *Atonement* was set, right through to the end, when – imagine! – you could have sex with people without having to meet their parents." The narrative style is traditional to match. "I wanted to draw on all the resources and fabulous roads laid down by the great nineteenth-century masters – that you can be in someone else's mind, you can restrict the horizon, you can decamp back into the head of the other person and see the two of them, or you can go right back and reflect on fate itself." In with Chekhov, then, and out with post-modern tricksiness.

The honeymoon night in *On Chesil Beach* is a minutely-observed catastrophe, but it's one so rooted in Edward and Florence's personal past as to become virtually inevitable. Those McEwanites (and there are many of them) who think that their man's fiction is always about unpredictable, transformative crises will need to think again. "I once agreed with something like this, and with the internet it's all out there, impossible to get back. Now I'll get Spanish or Portuguese journalists asking me 'Is always accident or crisis in your novel? Why is zis?' But look at *Atonement*, where I thought I was doing completely the opposite thing – there's 168 pages of unfolding story before we get to the key moment, the rape of a young girl. And now this act is shoehorned into this concept of 'the accidental', whereas in my terms there was a huge amount of pipework and draining and wiring laid down to get to it. I'm now bemused by this locked-in notion that I'm a writer of sudden catastrophes. Another thing people get wrong, a tiny thing really, is that someone must have asked me what I consider a minimum day's work and I would have answered about five hundred words. This found its way into the internet as fifteen words a day. Even a professional haiku writer would do more than that, even maybe a stonemason chiselling granite. But journalists from France and Germany think this is the ultimate badge of my mastery of language!"

A further misconception goes right back to 1970, when McEwan took an MA in English at the University of East Anglia, where he was taught by Malcolm Bradbury and Angus Wilson; the sole pupil in what is routinely described as Britain's first creative-writing course. "Eleven-twelfths of it was really just a standard English MA, with just a twelfth of it given over to creative writing – a piece of fiction rather than an essay. I wasn't really taught creative writing by Malcolm. I saw him just for a quarter of an hour, three times a year. But they were very important quarter-hours. He never told me what to do, never made suggestions. He just gave reading lists – which were really good – and I'd show him a story I'd been working on, he'd be encouraging, say something like 'I love that. When can I see the next one?' "

Ironically, after he left Norwich, McEwan became something of a poster boy for creative writing courses. He didn't mind too much, because his time at UEA had been both enjoyable and – with thirteen short stories completed on top of his normal MA essays – productive too. It gave him the confidence to think of himself as a writer in the first place; but what it didn't give him was any spoon-feeding. He's not sure how he would have handled the kind of creative writing teaching which has become commonplace since. "When I go to the States, I'm often asked to sit in on creative writing seminars where students' work is discussed at a length and depth I wouldn't have liked. I wanted to be left alone, not to have someone saying [putting on a whiny American accent] 'I have a problem with that character.' So I don't think I would have flourished in a real creative writing class." He didn't need to. He'd been given the space and encouragement to master his own technique, and already had the crucial element of self-discipline that all writers need. Perhaps this is a quality that comes from Scotland, and from his father David, who left school in Govan aged fourteen, lied about his age and joined the army.

At the end of *On Chesil Beach*, there are half a dozen pages in which McEwan runs fast-forward through Edward and Florence's subsequent lives. To imagine being Ian McEwan – which, no matter how quietly precise his answers or how wide-ranging his conversation, is always going to be a struggle – I suspect you have to flick across the decades in the other direction.

Start with an internationally successful author at the height of his powers; a writer who's always been fascinated by science. An author who wants to write about climate change, but hasn't yet worked out how to do so without it sounding preachy, but who talks about it both privately with experts (such as Al Gore) and publicly, as he did on stage in Hamburg last month with Germany's chief scientific adviser. Where did he get that from? Flick back a couple of years to that first holiday in Knoydart, or maybe that first walk on Chesil Beach. Back again, three more decades this time, to his father telling him his biggest regret was not studying science at university when the army offered him the chance. On the sound track, those words spooling into my tape recorder even now: "My love of science, my work ethic – I got it all from him." Back again, all the way to the Second World War, to his father's affair with his mother when she was married to a soldier who never came back home, to the story of the birth of his brother. Not a secret, maybe, but still, like *On Chesil Beach*, a story about a road not taken. Not something he'll write about now, but one day will, when he finally gets round to writing about David McEwan.

It's 1971. McEwan has finished studying at Norwich, but before he left he sold a short story – one of his first ever – to an American literary periodical. He used the money to go travelling, just another hippie in a psychedelic painted camper van, to Iran, Pakistan, Aghanistan. He kept a notebook all his time there, but has never written about it. Remember: he doesn't do autobiography, even in fiction. But it's there in our conversation all the same. "Homeric levels of hospitality. Incredibly welcoming people. Sitting on floors of people's homes sipping tea through crystallised sugar. The beautiful mosque in Herat. Kandahar before the wars..." And yet... "I had a colossal work ethic even then. It got buried in my six months on that journey. But there were times when I would just ache, just absolutely ache, to get back under grey skies in a bare whitewashed room. And I got all of that from him, from my father." A few months later, back in front of the typewriter in a whitewashed room in London, he's opening a package. *The New American Review.* Print run: 100,000. Publisher: Bantam. A garish pink cover, with a few names in white capitals on the front. Susan Sontag. Philip Roth. Ian McEwan. And, not being an omniscient narrator, that's where I'll stop.

P.S. - *Although* **On Chesil Beach** *didn't go on to win the 2007 Man Booker Prize, it did outsell all the other five shortlisted titles. It is available – along with all of Ian McEwan's previous fiction – in paperback from Vintage. Since this interview, the film of* **Atonement***, starring Keira Knightley, has been released to huge acclaim. It was nominated for seven Oscars, including Best Picture; and won two BAFTAs and an Academy Award. The libretto that Ian McEwan mentions he is writing is to* **For You***, a new opera about an ageing composer, with music by Michael Berkely.*

Janice Galloway

When I look back on this interview, I see I hardly asked any personal questions at all, that nearly everything is about her last novel, 'Clara'. I make no apologies for this. 'Clara' is, to my mind, the finest Scottish novel of the last decade, and in some ways Galloway's search for Clara Schumann trod a similar line between fact and fiction as my own search for Truman Capote. The difference is that while I looked at what journalism couldn't reveal, she showed what fiction could.

W HEN SHE discovered it, the house they had lived in wasn't imposing at all. Nothing special about it, quite small, no blue plaque on the wall, nothing to say that the great composer Robert Schumann had spent his last years of sanity here in Düsseldorf with his wife Clara and seven children. Upstairs, in the kitchen window, there was a light on. She could see a woman washing the dishes. Briefly, she thought of going up to the door and ringing the bell. She could explain, in her fractured German — what? That she was writing a book about Clara, a novel. She could ask the woman if she could see — what? The windowsill on which Robert had neatly laid out his shaving razors before asking Clara to call a carriage to take him to the asylum? The windows from which their children must have looked down at the street for their last sight of him? No, Janice Galloway decided. She wouldn't do that. She didn't need to. It was a novel she was writing, after all, not a biography.

Still, she wondered. She wondered about that time Robert had tried to commit suicide by throwing himself into the Rhine. How would he have got there from that house on Bilkerstrasse? She worked it out. There was only one way. He would have passed the statue of Our Lady, the pub on the corner, down a cobbled lane, to the river. A hundred and forty years later, she followed him. "If you stand there of an evening on the banks of the Rhine," she says, "and look across, there are just these tiny low lights. Cars, going slowly. But you can imagine them as carriages. And it was heart-stopping, that day, to stand there imagining that, how on a god-forsaken day a man was pushed to such an extremity that he did what he did."

One question not asked, one answer discovered. In some ways, that sets a pattern for Galloway's novel about Clara Schumann. If she didn't need to go inside the house at Bilkerstrasse, it is because she doesn't have an absolutely literal dependence on history. If she did need to walk down to the Rhine, it's because she depends hugely on an informed imagination. To Galloway, history is like that house. It offers the structure in which her subjects' lives were lived. Maybe if you peeled away at the wallpaper, you could even discover some faded part of their real background. But so what? To bring the past's lives to life, you need something more: the vital spark that Galloway was looking for, by the side of the river from which Robert Schumann was eventually rescued by fishermen. Empathy. Imagination. A Galloway novel, ever since her still-astounding 1989 debut novel *The Trick is to Keep Breathing*, is a guaranteed industrial-sized containerload of both.

We meet at her house in Dennistoun, Glasgow, and while the photographer is taking her picture, I browse her bookshelves in another room. Picking out a history of Robert Schumann, I read in it that historians can't work out whether his marriage to Clara was idyllic or a disaster. "Of course they can't," she says, "and it's certainly not for lack of source material. The Schumanns kept, for four years, a daily diary of their marriage. Robert kept a more intimate journal in which he recorded, among other things, how often they made love. There was a voluminous correspondence between them when Clara was away giving the piano recitals that made her one of the women celebrities of her century. And yet when it comes to knowing how happy their marriage really was, history has to be silent."

Thankfully, Janice Galloway doesn't. Thankfully, because this is a book she was born to write: a novel that seems to inhabit the minds of Clara and Robert Schumann so completely that you wonder why biography bothers. As, with typical forthrightness, does she. "Biography has always struck me as a bogus art," she says. "It is always a form of fiction, the way it sets its own priorities, the way it makes up its mind about a person. With Clara Schumann, there is obviously a repository of fact. But that's not a person. I can write down a repository of facts about my little boy [James, ten], but it wouldn't read like him, it wouldn't give the sensation of looking up and finding him in the room, it wouldn't show how he looks when he smiles. Even if you've got all the factual detail in the world, you're not describing a person. A person is their psychology, it's their memory, it's how things bounce off them, it's the sense of smell, the touch of their clothes ... "

Galloway colours in those people-sized gaps brilliantly. She takes us inside the mind of the Clara Schumanm we don't know: a five-year-old taught the piano because she was so silent her father wondered if she was deaf. Again, in most histories Clara's father is a background figure; in this novel, he's central. Galloway shows us precisely what it must have been like to be his child. To watch her mother drive away in a carriage and not know why, because divorce was almost as bad a social stigma as madness. To be drilled in the mechanics of music by her domineering father, pre-programmed to succeed like some nineteenth-century musical version of the tennis-playing Williams sisters. To fall in love with the young Robert, a pupil in her father's house. To marry against her father's wishes. To be a celebrity, touring from Dublin to Moscow. To be the mother of eight children. To wonder, all the time, about this man she has married. To fight his battles, even the biggest one, the one he can never win, the one for his sanity. And all the time, as this plot-heavy life unfolds, Galloway defiantly avoids using any of the signposts that normally mark out history. Until page 108, there's not a single date

("Still a bit too soon," she laughs). The Dresden Uprising of 1848 sweeps by, also dateless, its politics unexplained. So it's a mystery why there are these Prussian soldiers in town, why they want to arrest the young Wagner, and why Robert fears conscription. There are, in 423 pages, no conversations, no footnotes, precious little explanation about who the minor characters are and hardly anything about the times they are living through. It doesn't matter. Why should we expect voice-over narratives anyway? Instead, we live four decades in Clara's mind. We are shown how she and Robert share a love of musical ciphers, secrets and codes, and Robert, as a young student lodging with her father, tells her that a descending pattern of five notes will forever represent her name to him. We are told how they exchange notes – musical notes too – and how he interweaves that five-note pattern into his music and into their secret lives.

This is all superbly realised, in prose which, for all the book's length, never once turns stagnant with cliché. Behind it is a writer who seems not only to have mastered the trick of imagining her protagonists but – infinitely harder – of imagining their imagination as well. There are examples on every page, but here is just one. When cultural busybody Bettina von Arnim goes to visit Robert in his asylum (something Clara is expressly prohibited from doing by his doctors) she reproves Clara for allowing him to be in such a place. This is monstrously unfair, given that Clara spent half her lifetime as a surrendered wife, sacrificing herself for her husband; and the scenes of his final collapse are almost unbearably harrowing. "*Her only comfort,*" writes Galloway of Clara, "*was the hope that Frau von Arnim, in her finest silks, her perfume sparking the flames to pink, would one day burn in hell.*" Her perfume sparking the flames to pink. That small sentence shows us everything that history and biography can't manage: the inside of a mind, its poetry, its memories (with typical deftness, von Arnim's love of perfume has already been stealthily mentioned a decade or so earlier in Clara's life).

Even the most po-faced historian or biographer might accept that novelists are allowed that kind of latitude in dealing with their real-life subject's imagination. But what about the novelist who introduces letters and documents, the very stuff of history – undated, unsourced – into their own story? The novelist who makes up her own letters and hides them among the historical evidence so you can never know what is fiction and what is fact? Galloway gives a big round laugh at the thought of annoying the earnest cohorts of musicologists and biographers. "Oh yes, I've made up bits of letters and chopped others up. Sometimes I've joined several letters together, and in any case some of these are my translations and that's enough to make them fiction in itself." Does it matter? Normally, yes. If the basics of research have been ignored, if the author doesn't really care about the real-life subject, it could matter a lot. But not here. Galloway has done her homework, even though she doesn't let it dominate the book. In the six years it took her to write, she has read not only everything she could about the Schumanns but also as much as she could of all the authors who found their way into Robert or Clara's mind. Acres of Jean Paul Richter, reams of Robert's florid music criticism, as much of their contemporaries' music as she could get her ears on: all are clues clearly followed. Above all, she cares for Clara. She cares, because she knows how easily history overlooks women, how it is always the "bad boys" in music who command the attention, not the "good girls": the dutiful wives who gave up their own careers for their men; the quiet women who stayed at home, brought up the children and did all the work so their husbands could be great artists.

Robert Schumann suffered mental illness for most of his adult life, and this meant even more work for Clara. According to the American psychiatrist Peter Ostwald, Robert would now be diagnosed with a classic case of mania. "Reading his letters," says Galloway, "you can see the signs: the way he is casting around for someone to blame, the megalomania, spending money he didn't have, feelings of great power followed by feeling like shit. For me, though, the key to him is his early letters. He was so full of hope. Through the lens of history, it's possible to see him as just someone who died in a lunatic asylum, yet when you read his early letters, he's telling his mum what was happening right here, right now. He's so in the present moment, and it struck me that his illness had an attractive side too. Mania can be attractive – it shows through the skin when someone is getting high. Their skin glows, they talk all the time and look right into your eyes. It can be powerfully attractive until you realise it's not under control, that it can take all kinds of odd directions and become depressive."

According to one of the defining myths of the nineteenth century, madness is the flipside of creativity. "That's a stupid, elitist notion," says Galloway, "that idea that people who create are somehow special and that they've got a layer of skin less. You can't create anything when you're in the throes of black depression or extreme mania. When you look at it the next day, it's junk. Schumann always knew the difference between what he had written under the influence of mania and the really good stuff. He was such a gentle man, although at the mercy of his illness. Some of his songs cannot be equalled by anyone."

The first time she ever heard a Schumann song, Galloway says, was when her former partner, Graham McNaught, sang them to her. "Graham is, quite simply, the best pianist this country has ever produced. He sang "*Frauenliebe und Leben*" ("Woman's Love and Life") to me. It was such a privilege. It blew me away." For a moment, she falls silent, remembering. Behind the beauty of the song's music, though, its words were dusty with antique meanings. For the woman in the song, for example, life only starts with the love of a man, and it ends when he dies. At one point, Galloway worked on "feminising" the songs. "With [the composer] Sally Beamish, what I wanted to do was to write words that would put the real woman, the real Clara, into the eight-song cycle. That would have lasted hours, so in 1995 we boiled it down to just one song, which tries to encapsulate everything about her. I always knew though that I'd go back and use the same idea." So here, "*Frauenliebe und Leben*" forms Clara's musical framework. It must, I suggest, have made its writing easier. "In some ways, it was an enormous frustration, because you've got to stay true to the life. You might have a wonderful idea, but you're not allowed to do it. There were times when I thought, 'Why did I pick this? If only I'd picked Jane Stirling!'" Seeing the incomprehension on my face, she explains that Stirling was a Scottish woman who fell in love with Chopin on his British tour. He called her his "tedious Scottish girl"; she convinced herself she could make him love her, and baked him scones before obligingly falling off the footnotes of history into total obscurity.

With Clara Schumann, however, there are so many more notes that have to be attached to the past's stave, so many more apparent restrictions on the imagination. The discipline of staying close to a real life has to be that much more rigorous, you might have thought it would stifle creativity altogether. But somehow, it hasn't worked like that. The book's discipline actually helps it. You read *Clara* and you catch the music of another mind, and wherever it comes from – the banks of the Rhine in Düsseldorf, a song cycle heard in a Glasgow house, or the music teacher at Ardrossan Academy to whom this book is dedicated – Janice Galloway plays the notes to what sounds very much like perfection. As one would expect from Clara Schumann herself, this is a virtuosa performance.

P.S. - *All of Janice Galloway's fiction is available in Vintage paperback. More information about her work, and details of forthcoming readings and events, can be found at the website www.galloway.1to1.org. In 2008, Janice Galloway became the first Scottish recipient of the Jura Writers' Fellowship. At the Hunterian Gallery in Glasgow, her collaboration with visual artist Anne Bevan – a piece incorporating text and sculpture, entitled "Rosengarten" – is now on permanent display.*

William Dalrymple

He's Scotland's best travel writer, and perhaps, its best historian too. He has found his subject in the Mughal empire, and he lives for half the year with his wife and three children near Delhi, its old capital. His 2002 book 'White Mughals' argued the case for the multi-cultural roots of the British Empire in late eighteenth-century India; in 'The Last Mughal' (2006) he looked at how that more tolerant world ended in the arrogance of the Raj and the bloody repression of the Indian Mutiny.

I T'S JUNE 2, 2003, and I am in William Dalrymple's garden, on the day his life starts to turn around. The previous day had begun with the bank manager on the phone, pointedly noting that he'd done nothing about paying back his £27,000 overdraft: that all the requisite warnings had been issued and that financially dire consequences were just a day or so away. Four hours later, another telephone call. It's the organisers of the Wolfson History Prize, ringing to tell him he's won £10,000 for *White Mughals*, his spellbinding story of the love between an English ambassador and an Indian princess at the end of the eighteenth century. And I'm in his garden now because I know the book's just won the £10,000 Scottish Arts Council Book of the Year Award, and I'm writing a feature about him.

We don't know the half of it then, William Dalrymple and I, as we sit out in the sun outside his Queen Anne cottage in Chiswick. We don't know that *White Mughals* will go on to be one of the first books chosen for Richard and Judy's Book Club; that its sales will double to 200,000 as a result; that plans will be drawn up for a film; that a stage adaptation (by Christopher Hampton, no less) will be staged at the National Theatre, and a film version may well follow. We don't yet know that he will leave his current publisher for Bloomsbury, who will offer him an astronomical deal for his next six books; a deal that will keep him working for the next twenty years, writing a history of the rise, decline and fall of India's Mughal empire.

Sitting in his oddly peaceful garden, somehow isolated from the Heathrow-bound traffic roaring up the Great West Road nearby, he tells me what he is going to write about next. It will be another Indian story, but one "like Stalingrad set in Renaissance Florence". Stalingrad because it will show how the Victorian British tore apart the contentedly multi-racial society of eighteenth-century India, putting down the Indian Mutiny with a violence that shudders across the centuries. Florence because the world they destroyed was the last great flowering of Mughal culture in Delhi. He will call it *The Last Mughal*, and already he knows exactly where it will begin: in Rangoon on a rainy September night in 1862. The last Mughal emperor, whose ancestors included Genghis Khan and Tamerlaine, the great Babur who had conquered India three centuries ago, and Shah Jahan, who built the Taj Mahal, is being buried in a lime-drenched plywood coffin in a pauper's grave. There is no ceremony, no monument, not even a simple gravestone. The British officer in charge makes sure the turf is carefully replaced so "there will be no surviving vestige to mark the remains of the great Mughals". It's a good story, I say feebly. "It's a f***ing great story," says William Dalrymple, throwing back his head and laughing.

❖   ❖   ❖

It's August 2006, and William Dalrymple breezes into the café where we've arranged to meet, not too far from his parents' house near North Berwick. To breeze, it strikes me, is the perfect Dalrymple verb. He exudes breeziness; and is affable, bright, lively, exhilarating company every time I meet him. A few weeks before, I'd seen him at the Borders Book Festival in Melrose. His event was packed out, it was time to start, and there he was, strolling up the road outside, late because he'd been watching *Doctor Who* with his three children. He breezed in, unperturbed, unconcerned, unruffled. He breezed through a bravura reading of his books: first the award-winning travel books, starting with *In Xanadu*, which he wrote at the age of 22, then on to the ground-breaking history of the *White Mughals*, a brief summary of the new book, a breezy grin at the applauding crowd, and off he breezed again. It's a deceptive word, though, breeziness. It masks effort, discipline, emotion, scholarship. Look beneath the panache, the seemingly effortless style with which Dalrymple writes his history, and you see something else. When, at Melrose, he read out a letter from the daughter of the Indian princess Khair-un-Nissa, now back in England, to the grandmother in India she hadn't seen for three decades, there was a catch in his voice, a slight watering in his eyes.

You have to read *White Mughals* to understand why. And, once you've read it, you have to understand how intensely he researched the story of the Indian princess's love. His young daughter once caught me looking at the portrait of Khair-un-Nissa on the wall of his study. "That's Daddy's girlfriend," she told me solemnly, and for the amount of time and money Dalrymple spent finding out about her, she might as well have been. Before he began his research, what was known about Khair-un-Nissa's marriage could have been written in a couple of paragraphs and summed up by a few local rumours in Hyderabad. In the book he was originally writing, about multi-culturalism in eighteenth-century India, it wouldn't have made much more. But everything changed when Dalrymple, like a literary Indiana Jones, tracked down a hitherto-untapped source that told the story in full.

Tracing that ribbon of romance across the centuries, finding out what happened to the children of the ambassador and the princess would, he realised, take another year or so of research. The money would run out, of course, but so what? The children would have to be taken out of prep school. If it came to it, they could always sell up and move to India. And why not? Hadn't Dalrymple known, for more than twenty years, that one day he would? That they'd live in

Delhi: himself, his wife Olivia, and their three children – not just to write a book (as he did for his 1996 *City of Djinns*) – but because it felt right? That he, solidly Scottish to his ancestral aristocratic roots, would one day find himself, for nine months of the year, tapping out books on a computer in his garden pavilion while the bulbuls and hoopoes sang and the parrots squawked outside? Hadn't he imagined that?

❖   ❖   ❖

It's 26 January 1984, and eighteen-year-old William Dalrymple is on a bus, going past the Red Fort in New Delhi. It's the day his life changes, when it splits into "before" and "after". Before, he'd never been outside Britain except for a trip to Paris with his mother, and this makes India's impact all the more dramatic. Here he is, on his first day there, and it feels as if he's just arrived on another planet. Out of the bus window, he notices the thousand-yard-long red sandstone palace, and maybe wonders what kind of people once lived there. He doesn't know, then, that it was built by the Shah Jahan at the height of the Mughal empire in the seventeenth century ("*If there be paradise on earth*," said the inscription on the dais beneath the Peacock Throne, "*it is here*"), or that, even in the days of the last emperor, the poetry recitals, dancing and ghazal singing would go on there until 3.30am, just a couple of hours before the British would start their day; praying, riding and walking in the cool of dawn. And he definitely doesn't know that one day he'll write a book about the last emperor's life in the Red Fort, and how he became the leader of the biggest challenge the British empire at its mightiest ever faced; that once again he'll discover an untapped source that will help him rewrite the Indian Mutiny, and that when he does, the words will pour out of him "like a torrent" – at such a rate that the whole book will only take him five months to write. Dalrymple's books are big ("like their author, my books are getting bulkier with age", he grins), and such speed is all the more astonishing considering the narrative panache and ambition of his work, which makes most other historians seem little more than revisionist tinkerers.

In other accounts of the Indian Mutiny, there's not much about the insurgents. British historians would shrug and say the sources didn't exist. Indian historians never looked too hard, because the mutineers' aims of restoring a Muslim emperor – one whose court records were in a barely decipherable late Mughal notation of Urdu – hardly squares with the kind of straightforward nationalistic history that modern India secretly wishes it had. Because what actually happened in 1857 wasn't a mass rising against a colonial power, but Hindu soldiers fighting to put a Muslim on the throne to rule over them. Imagine an Irish Easter Rising in which the Catholics fought to put Protestant landlords back in power, and you get some idea of the historiographical confusion the Mutiny can cause in India today. The new book, Dalrymple knows, won't make him popular there. "The nationalist interpretation is that the sepoys [mutineers] and the people fought on the same side. What we found out also shows the people and the sepoys and the British in a three-cornered contest, with the sepoys fighting the British but also raiding the grain stores and antagonising the people. It's a picture of complete chaos and dissension." Dalrymple's sources had been overlooked, he says, because they are not in either English or Hindi, the two main languages of modern middle-class India. But there are, he discovered, plenty of records of the Mughals and the mutineers: hundreds and hundreds of boxes full, and right where you'd expect to find them, filed and catalogued in the National Archives of India in 1921, but hardly touched since. "The detail is incredible," says Dalrymple. "There's every police station record, every court report, everyone from the Durbar of the Great Mughal, from every level of society. The British collected every bit of paper they could find in the royal palace or the sepoys' camp with a view to using it all in trials after the mutiny was crushed. It's as if you'd only heard of Stalingrad from the Nazi side, and you suddenly come across all the Russian archives. And at the moment, I seem to be the only person doing this."

There are two main requirements for a compelling history, he reckons: a well-documented and interesting subject, and one with a narrow enough focus, so you can tell the story in the kind of detail that novelists do. A third, he adds, is a good editor: his own, Michael Fishwick, fits the bill perfectly. Yet now, with his projected five-volume history of the Mughal empire, Dalrymple is widening, rather than narrowing, the canvas. After that first trip to India, he returned to Britain to study at Cambridge, where he discovered the works of Sir Steven Runciman, the supreme historian of Byzantium and the Crusades, who also lived in Scotland, also travelled the world and also always gave Islamic culture its proper weight in his histories. "His great Crusades trilogy has always had pride of place on my bookshelves," says Dalrymple, "and I think it would be very nice to be able to leave a great lump of books like his behind, even if it takes me twenty years." But won't he lose his readership? I ask. After all, *White Mughals* had an irresistible love story at its heart, and also showed us, for the first time, that eighteenth-century India was, in his words, "an infinitely more culturally, racially and religiously mixed place than modern Britain can even dream of being". *The Last Mughal* reveals the other side of the story – an imperial power grown arrogant, contemptuous of other cultures and repressive – and might also be seen to have contemporary echoes. But how many of his readers will follow him back into sixteenth-century India, the height of Mughal power, when the comparatively poor, unsophisticated British traders couldn't imagine gaining so much as a foothold on the sub-continent?

He's not having any of it. "The Mughals are extraordinary people. First you have Babur, who's an extraordinarily humane, engaging, self-critical personality, yet who also conquers India. Then you have this opium addict who loses his father's empire, but his son Akbar I can't wait to write about. This is a man who, when the

Inquisition was in full swing in Europe, called representatives of every religious faith, even atheists, to his capital and told them everyone would be free to believe what they wanted. Then there's Aurangzeb, who brings it all crashing down again because everything's been based on the alliances with the Hindus that Akbar made, and ... honestly, it's a great, great story."

He said that to me once before, and he was right then, too. So here's a prediction, made even more certain by the fact that he writes beautifully, and he's got an entire civilisation to himself: what Edward Gibbon was to ancient Rome, William Dalrymple will be to the magnificent Mughals. A funkier Gibbon, perhaps; definitely, a breezier one.

P.S. - *William Dalrymple has a website at www.williamdalrymple.uk.com. His travel books –* **In Xanadu, City of Djinns, From the Holy Mountain,** *and* **The Age of Kali,** *are all available in paperback from Flamingo.* **White Mughals** *is published in paperback by HarperCollins, and* **The Last Mughal** *by Bloomsbury.*

William Boyd

If Truman Capote was trying to write the "non-fiction novel" with 'In Cold Blood', much of William Boyd's writing goes in the opposite direction. In 'The New Confessions', he gave us a fictional autobiography, in 'Nat Tate: American Artist' he produced a fictional biography, and in 'Any Human Heart' he wrote the fictional intimate journal. I talked to him about it — and about the "large, blurry border where fiction stops and fact begins" — in his Chelsea home in 2002, just before publication of 'Any Human Heart'.

W ILLIAM BOYD has kept a journal for most of his life. He knows how they work: those declamatory opening paragraphs, those high hopes, that late-adolescent intensity. And he knows how odd it all looks now, how distant; the way you don't recognise the face you see in the mirror these days, these thirty years later. He was nineteen when he started. Home was Ghana, the family were Fifers, school had been Gordonstoun, university was Glasgow. He read English, got a First, met his wife, went on to do a DPhil at Oxford. Yet when he looks back, when he reads his journal entries from the early 1970s, he says he doesn't recognise himself. "I am surprised at just how neurotic I seemed to be," he says with a languid smile.

Neurotic is not the kind of adjective anyone would dream of associating with him now. Urbane, yes: the house in Chelsea, the house in the South of France, the month a year he spends in New York. Certain, certainly: anyone who not only writes for the screen, but also directs his own films, has to be. Successful, absolutely: not just the £200,000 advances in the UK, but automatic bestseller status in France as well. British literary fiction is rarely this popular. But it is Boyd's journal, threading its way back to that long-forgotten, neurotic student self, that is the key to his latest novel, *Any Human Heart*. It, too, takes the form of a writer's journal. Logan

Mountstuart, born in Uruguay in 1906 and educated at an English public school, is wildly successful as a writer in the 1920s, and marries the daughter of an aristocrat. In successive decades he is a blissfully happy suburban divorcé, a spy of sorts in the war, a New York art dealer, an academic in Africa, and a pensioner living in penury in a London basement. The key doesn't lie in any parallels between the lives of the two writers. Forget the fact that both of them are artloving, upper middle-class outsiders, and disregard the shared boarding-school background. It's simpler than that. Here, form governs content, and the form – a fictitious journal, deliciously laced with real-life references – is one that Boyd has virtually to himself.

Quite why this should be so is a mystery, and Boyd's novel must make many writers realise just how many tricks they've been missing. A journal is deeper than a diary; the place to try out voices and ideas more deliberately – and is, after all, where we record what we really think about other people, and about ourselves. It takes us straight to, well, any human heart. In it, we make endless false starts and a few real ones. We repeat ourselves, make appalling jokes and inadvertently give away our prejudices. We try out new styles of writing and then lose our nerve, or realise we are just being pretentious. And even when we don't, our style of writing alters slowly over the years, as the years effect their changes upon us. Most novels can only show a small part of this. They have plots, omniscient narrators, ominous hints about what the future may bring: everything that real life doesn't. "The intimate journal is the only literary form that imitates the way we experience being human," says Boyd. "Unlike biography, it does not look for patterns to try to make sense of life; unlike autobiography, it does not endlessly look back on life. We don't live like that."

There's another advantage to this form of fiction: it's an easy one to dress up as fact. But to make this work, each verifiable piece of history has to be dropped on to the stream of recorded life as carefully and unobtrusively as an angler placing a fly on the surface of a river. If you can see the ripples, it's not going to work. In Boyd's hands, the fly lands gently on the water. Here's an example. When Logan Mountstuart is in Paris in the 1920s, he meets Ernest Hemingway. The circumstances are altogether plausible. Mountstuart isn't impressed and tells his journal why: Hem had been drinking with an American friend and was mocking the Brit's posh accent. The next day, when they meet in the Boulevard St Germain, Hemingway apologises. It's just, he explains, the presence of one friend in particular makes him "*roaring and meanly drunk*". The footnote tells us whom we have just inadvertently encountered. "*F Scott Fitzgerald (1896-1940) was in Paris at the time.*" Gradually, the stage fills up with people we either know or think we know from history. Virginia Woolf is encountered at Garsington (along with Leonard Woolf and Aldous Huxley: the authenticating footnote reads "*See The Diary of Virginia Woolf Vol III 1925-30*"); James Joyce is helped to discover a word he will later use in *Finnegans Wake*; and Ian Fleming, working in naval intelligence, gives Mountstuart a job. As naval attaché, Mountstuart earns the enmity of the Duke and Duchess of Windsor, and reveals why he suspects the Duke of perverting the course of justice over the murder of Harry Oakes, a millionaire tax exile in the Bahamas in 1943. Each tendril of fact introduced to the story latches itself on, and buds into new life with succeeding journal entries. Before long, the boundaries between fact and fiction are completely and brilliantly overgrown.

Ever since *The New Confessions*, his similarly epic fictionalised autobiography, this has been the most obvious feature of Boyd's work. Four years ago, his "biography" of a non-existent American artist called Nat Tate not only hoaxed the New York art world, it led to a twenty-minute *Newsnight* disquisition on the nature of biographical truth. In that book, Logan Mountstuart, as a New York art dealer in the 1950s, was one of Tate's main supporters. In this one, with its ten-page index, literary games of Borgesian complexity are also being played. But are they just games? Boyd's short answer is no: sometimes fiction tells the facts better. "You're putting beautiful lies in the service of truth," he says. "Obviously, I never met the Duke and Duchess of Windsor, for example, but I feel as though I've got them pinned down, that they really must have been revolting. Yet I only wrote what I did after fairly extensive research. As a novelist, I can then take that extra step a little closer to reality." That's neat and straightforward, not as controversial as it might seem. But on the walls of Boyd's house in Chelsea are at least two other answers. I don't notice the three Keith Vaughan sketches of male nudes until he starts talking about them, about how he started collecting British artists from the late 1940s and early 1950s when he first came to London. There were other, greater names - the Graham Sutherland over the fireplace is, he says, his pride and joy - but Vaughan retains a special place in Boyd's affections. For one thing, both men are writers as well as artists. Boyd's hand-drawn storyboards for his film *The Trench*, which his wife Susan had bound in a sumptuous leather album, show a fine eye for linear form. At school, influenced by the charismatic art teacher who also taught Prince Charles (and who still keeps in touch with both of them), he wanted to be a painter when he grew up. But for parental opposition, he might have been. Like Logan Mountstuart, Keith Vaughan attempted to commit suicide in 1977. Unlike Mountstuart, he succeeded. "But the journals he wrote are the most candid I think anyone's ever written. He was unhappy, misanthropic, was gay and had a very weird sexuality, but his journals have such an honesty that they are one of the influences on the book."

For a second, let's look closer at Mountstuart. He is, says Boyd, an amalgam of Cyril Connolly and William Gerhardie. Connolly, the great perfectionist of English letters was also, by his own standards, a colossal failure. And Gerhardie, like Mountstuart, was a hot young novelist in the 1920s, who spent the last 37 years of his life in gradually increasing poverty, unable to find a publisher. These might seem unlikely influences. Everything about Boyd's career, by contrast, positively screams success. This is a man, after all, who has written scripts for eight feature films, who has directed his own, who even now is working on a drama for TV about Hitler's early life. His novels have a huge range, dynamism and virtuosity, each one radically different from the last, from his 1981 debut *A Good Man in Africa* right through to *Any Human Heart*. What has any of that to do with failure?

But listen to him talking about Gerhardie's long slide into obscurity and you suspect that his fear of failure is real enough. In his day, Gerhardie was just as fêted as Boyd ("I have talent, you have genius," Evelyn Waugh told him), yet he ended up unread and hopelessly unfashionable. "He's the great warning about how, in the writing business, things can always go terribly pear-shaped," says Boyd. And then you remember those passages in *Any Human Heart* where Mountstuart bemoans his fate; when his journal entries point out that no biographies of writers ever cover their descent into oblivion. You remember Mountstuart's own interest in a group of French poets called the Cosmopolitans: the acme of style and sophistication in the years leading up to the First World War, and completely neglected thereafter. Even the Nat Tate hoax itself was based on the premise that a young genius artist of the 1950s could reasonably expect to be ignored forty years on.

So you look up at this writer in front of you, who works hard and intelligently and successfully across three media, the kind of writer who gets invited for meet-the-Prince weekends at Sandringham, and who has such a way with narrative that most critics have to reach back to Graham Greene for a comparison. Not the most likely candidate, you would have thought, to fear failure. Then you recall the Henry James quote the novel takes its title from: "*Never say that you know the last word about any human heart.*" And you wonder.

P.S. - **Any Human Heart** *was subsequently shortlisted for the International IMPAC Dublin Literary Award, and in 2005, William Boyd received the CBE. In 2006, Boyd's latest novel,* **Restless**, *won the Costa Award for Best Novel, and in the following year, was shortlisted for the Richard & Judy Best Read of the Year at the British Book Awards.* **Restless***, which follows the life of Russian emigré Eva from her recruitment to the British Secret Service in 1939, to her attempt to rebuild her life as an English wife and mother after the War, is available in paperback from Bloomsbury. All of William Boyd's previous fiction is published by Penguin.*

Looking For Mma Ramotswe

I never did get to meet the woman Alexander McCall Smith was think-ing of when he wrote his first story about Mma Ramotswe, the owner of the No. 1 Ladies' Detective Agency, but I know she does exist — or that she did when I visited Botswana with him four years ago. But although I must have passed right past her house without knowing it, I did at least, like Mma Ramotswe herself, make a few surprising sleuthing discoveries of my own...

THE MAIN problem with looking for the most famous woman in Botswana is that she's almost entirely fictional. Beyond the imagination of Alexander McCall Smith and the five million people who have bought his novels, there really is no large-hearted private detective called Mma Ramotswe, no matter how we might yearn for such a palpably decent, kindly sorter-out of other people's problems. At the foot of Kgale Hill, there is no No. 1 Ladies' Detective Agency*. On Gaborone's bustling Twokleng Road, there is no Speedy Motors Garage, where Mr JLB Matekoni, fiction's most charming mechanic and Mma Ramotswe's adoring husband, plies his oily craft. You already know that there won't be, even as you fly into Gaborone airport with the fanciful aim of sleuthing out the "real" Mma Ramotswe. And when you drive from there to the centre of Botswana's capital, on roads thronged with gleaming flatbed trucks, it seems even more of a fool's errand. Those miles of ultra-modern trading estates and offices marking out Africa's fastest-growing city; those long avenues of bungalows, their walls tipped with electric fences; that mall across the road, with shoppers edging past luxury sports cars and fashion shows to pour into the hi-fi shops; the cinema multiplexes showing the same films as they do in Britain — everything you see tells you you're wasting your time: Mma Ramotswe couldn't possibly live in a place as thor-oughly westernised, as relentlessly up-to-the-minute, as this. But

Although there is, from July 2008, a No.1 Ladies' Opera House

you're wrong. You've just got to look harder, that's all. And when you do, you're in for a whole string of surprises.

It's Sunday, 7:30am on a clear Botswanan winter's day in 2004, and I am in church. The Anglican cathedral of the Holy Cross in Gaborone is where Mma Ramotswe worships her God, kneeling at pews facing a large altar table. Long strips of red light fall across the congregation's faces from the stained-glass windows behind it. The reading is *II Kings 5:1-15*, the story about how the king of Syria asks the king of Israel to heal his best general, Na'aman, "a mighty man, but a leper". The king of Israel takes this as a de facto declaration of war. He can't possibly heal Na'aman ("Am I God, to kill and make alive?"). The prophet Elijah, however, can and does, and Na'aman's "flesh is restored like the flesh of a little child, and he was clean". I look around at the congregation. If the statistical averages of the population apply equally to the worshippers, then one out of every two women in their twenties in the pews behind me will die of AIDS. One in three Botswanans aged between 15 and 45 has HIV, the highest incidence of the virus in the world. Imagine that: the crowds in Gaborone's Africa Square, the shoppers in the River Walk malls, the packed stands for the Zebras' soccer games. One in three. About the same number as those upon whose upturned faces the light falls through the stained-glass windows in the cathedral.

Behind the altar, Howard Moffat is taking the service. A friend of McCall Smith's since their teenage years in colonial Rhodesia, he appears briefly in every one of the *No. 1 Ladies' Detective Agency* books. A doctor as well as a minister, he is the medical superintendent at Gaborone's main hospital and personal physician to Botswana's president. He is also, says McCall Smith, the nearest thing he knows to a saint. Moffat is a reserved, gentle, quiet-spoken man, and there is indeed an aura of goodness about him. Perhaps I'm only thinking that because I know his hospital has the biggest AIDS clinic in the world, and a doctor I know who visited him there came away humbled by his colossal workload. But perhaps not: one of the reasons McCall Smith's books are so successful is that they acknowledge the reality of goodness in a way so little contemporary fiction does – both in the hard work of real people like Howard Moffat, and in the life of Mma Ramotswe.

Long before AIDS came to Botswana, Howard Moffat was a busy man. In Mochudi, the village thirty-five miles away, in which Mma Ramotswe grew up, he used to be the head of the local hospital. In the books, McCall Smith has him treating Obed, Mma Ramotswe's father, as he lay dying of a lung disease contracted when working in South Africa's gold mines. He'd probably have treated Mma Ramotswe too. In fact – and this is where the boundary with fiction almost dissolves – that's just what he did.

Alexander McCall Smith has often spoken about how he first got the idea of writing about a woman like Mma Ramotswe. It's a simple, apparently insignificant, story. In 1980, he was visiting Howard and Fiona Moffat in Mochudi, and was walking with Fiona in the village late one summer afternoon when a large lady called out to her. She wanted, she said, to give Dr Moffat a chicken. She chased it round the yard, wrung its neck, and handed it over. That's it. End of story. Or rather, the start of one, because fifteen years later, sitting in front of his computer in Edinburgh, McCall Smith thought back to that woman, to how eager she had been to give his friend that present, how she had bustled around her clean-swept yard with such determination. He started writing a story of a woman like her, a woman whose father had died, and who had decided to set up a detective agency. End of story again. It had only taken four pages. But he found himself wondering, as writers do, about the life of that woman whom he had only seen for a few minutes. And the more he thought about her, the more it seemed to fit in with memories of 1981, the year he'd spent in Botswana setting up the law faculty of its only university.

McCall Smith loves the country with a passion that can perhaps only come from someone born in Africa. Back then, Botswana's virtues shone more brightly against the horrors of apartheid, only thirty miles away across the South African border. But this land, this Botswana, was a completely colour-blind country, whose first president had risked everything for the love of the white woman he married; a democracy, free of corruption, observing the rule of law, almost free of crime, with an unfettered press; a country which had never been invaded or riven by tribal fighting, where guns were banned and the police unarmed – and where the world's biggest source of gem diamonds had been found, on the edges of the Kalahari, just a year after the British pulled out in 1966. In short, almost a paradise. So he returned to Mma Ramotswe, this good woman in a good country, and wrote the first book in a series whose popularity encircles the globe. Mma Ramotswe is not the woman who chased the chicken round her clean-swept yard in Mochudi, but without the one, we might never have had the other. So here's the question: Who is that woman who inadvertently provided the inspiration for McCall Smith's novels?

Until now, no-one has known. The "real" Mma Ramotswe is now 73, extremely deaf, possibly confused about her accidental role in literature, and unwilling to be interviewed by strangers like me – so we'll give her the name Mma Betty. She still lives in Mochudi, where Dr Moffat treated her for diabetes. She no longer keeps chickens, but grows gourds and squash in her yard, some of which she sells to neighbours. And when friends of mine visited her for an hour last week, she welcomed them in, sat them all down in her overcrowded lounge and did exactly what the fictional Mma Ramotswe would also have done immediately: offered them tea and cake. Mma Betty was shorter than she used to be, but just as large – "traditionally built" in McCall Smith's endearing euphemism – as ever. She opened the door wearing a large tartan headscarf and grubby glasses, apologising for the small amount of building work in her yard. "Welcome to my ruin," she said, laughing, ushering her visitors into a lounge crammed with three unmatching settees, various other chairs, and a cluttered dining-room table. On the walls were the certificates she'd been awarded for her work as a teacher and leader of the Sunbeams, as Brownies are called in Botswana; a picture of Botswana's first president, Sir Seretse Khama, and one of her only son. No, she said, she didn't recall chasing that chicken to give to Dr Moffat, or meeting the man whose stories she had accidentally inspired. My friends gave her a copy of *The No. 1 Ladies' Detective Agency*. She promised to read it.

The real truths from which fiction is woven are like that: they come from a different angle to the written story. Remember that first lesson from the Bible at the Cathedral of the Holy Cross, which I thought had been specially chosen because of the parallels between leprosy and AIDS? It wasn't: in every Anglican service in the world, that was the text for the Sunday on which I heard it. Now it's three days later, and I'm in a car with Derek James, the charismatic 62-year-old director of a charity which runs two orphanages in Botswana. We are heading west towards the border with South Africa, the country he left 32 years ago, when the pressures of being an ANC supporter and defying the cruel absurdities of apartheid grew too great. I wanted to see the SoS Children's Village at Twokleng, the "orphan farm" in McCall Smith's series, because this is where Mma Ramotswe's children come from, and because its former matron is another real-life person with a role in the novels. Although I don't know it yet, I am travelling behind the fiction, towards an even stranger truth.

In McCall Smith's series, Mma Ramotswe's fiancé, the estimable Mr JLB Matekoni, is a regular visitor to the orphanage. Each time he goes there, Mma Potokwane, its formidable matron, inveigles him into fixing any machinery that needs attention, or repairing the orphanage's trucks and its battered minibus. *In Tears of the Giraffe*, Mma Potokwane tells Mr JLB Matekoni the story of the two most recent arrivals at the orphanage. A band of nomadic Kalahari bushmen had been on an ostrich-hunt when one of the mothers died. According to bushman custom, when this happens, if the mother is still feeding a baby, it is buried with her. A baby boy had been wrapped up in animal hide and buried alive in a shallow, sandy grave. His sister, who was five years old, had hidden in the bush, and when the adults had moved on, she dug up her baby brother and ran off with him in her arms. When she reached a road, a passer-by took them both to Francistown hospital, near the border with Zimbabwe. The baby was still alive. The children learnt Setswana and were given foster parents in the town, but then the girl who had rescued her brother was struck down by TB of the spine. She was now in a wheelchair, and when her foster parents could no longer cope, she and her brother were sent to the orphanage. It's an important part of the story, because these are children JLB Matekoni will take home and Mma Ramotswe will adopt: the wheelchair-bound Motholeli and her younger brother Puso. But that's all I had assumed it was: a story. I'd never imagined it might be true. "Sure it is," says Derek James. "Every bit of it — apart from the fact that they're both girls. If you want, I can show you the files."

There are terrible stories in these files. A boy whose stepfather put him in a hut and set it on fire when he was one year old. An eight-year-old girl who had been tied to a tree at the back of a she-been and used as a sex object. Seven children with full-blown AIDS. You flick through the official trail of these brief lives — the social workers' recommendations, the medical case notes, the care histories — and the pictures attached. All the children are beaming at the camera — except, at first, little Khumo. She would have been one year old when she was buried alive by her tribe, nine by the time she was admitted to the orphanage in 1990. In the first picture, you can tell that she really is trying to force a small grin for the camera, but she can't. Even her case notes admit that "she doesn't find it easy to smile". She's shy, note the house mothers at the orphanage; she doesn't like talking, and she is far better at football than anything else at school.

Karabo is three years older. She was six when she dug up her little sister, cleared the sand from her mouth and nose and carried her to safety. The two girls lived for a while at the hospital near the huge diamond mine at Orapa, then were fostered to a family near Francistown. It didn't work out. The foster parents were unemployed and started neglecting them; particularly when, at the age of nine, Karabo got TB and had to start using a wheelchair. At the Twokleng orphanage, though, she blossomed. She was popular, friendly, outgoing. After she left the orphanage, a place was found for her at a workshop for physically disabled adults forty miles away, where she assembled solar rechargeable hearing aids, before being promoted to receptionist. Three years ago, following a relationship with a co-worker, she had a baby. Khumo only left the orphanage last year, when she turned 21. After going to hotel school in Namibia, she is now a waitress in a motel only a short walk away. It's a poorly paid job: only £55 a month, and the orphanage is still helping her by paying her rent.

These, then, are the true stories of fictional people. It's no surprise that they only overlap at the start. If they echoed each other completely – if, for example, Motholi and Puso stayed on at the orphanage, as Karabo and Khumo did, or if Mma Ramotswe really was Mma Betty – McCall Smith's books would be very different. And yes, it would certainly be possible to paint an altogether bleaker portrait of Botswana: one that shows its rising crime rate, the effect of AIDS, and unemployment far higher than the official figures of nineteen per cent. But these books are about something more than social realism. They are gently paced, charming stories where good things usually happen to good people: in the latest Mma Ramotswe novel, for example, a decent ex-convict is given a second chance, our heroine's own honesty saves her from blackmail, and her physically rather unprepossessing assistant accidentally discovers love with a patently decent man. Real life, we might say to ourselves, isn't like that. But we suspend our disbelief because McCall Smith makes such a convincing case that, in a good country like Botswana at least, it just might be. My first impressions, as I drove from Gaborone airport, were that this was a country whose anodyne modernity might just as easily be anywhere else, and I felt slightly disillusioned. Only out in the villages on the way to the Kalahari did life start to resemble what I had imagined: thatched rondavels, traditionally built women, a palpably slower pace.

Gradually, I started to notice how wrong those first impressions were: that even in the city, people's friendliness exceeded my expectations. After church, for example, the congregation applauded me just for coming from Scotland, and complete strangers invited me into their house for lunch. In the streets, casual greetings were given by passers-by as a matter of course. In conversation, there was a greater attentiveness to the speaker, an easiness of laughter. Maybe McCall Smith is right; maybe this really is a place where goodness happens that bit more readily.

On my last night, there was a party at the Moffats' house. By that stage, I'd seen a lot more of the country than most visitors will, from a brunch on the well-watered lawns of the State House to nights under the stars of the Kalahari, where the members of our small safari team were the only humans in an area the size of Portugal. I'd talked to Botswanan writers and orphans, seen the world's largest HIV research clinic outside America and, like Mma Ramotswe, I'd drunk bush tea on the veranda of the President's Hotel. I'd met a lot of people I liked a great deal. But now my search for Mma Ramotswe was winding down to a close. In the garden of the Moffat house, which Mma Ramotswe visits in the latest book after giving a lift to Fiona Moffat (*"because in Botswana, no-one passes a friend"*), under a large spreading jacaranda tree, many of the people I'd met in the course of the week were already gathered. Rev. Trevor Mwamba*, the irrepressibly charming priest who marries Mma Ramotswe to JLB Matekoni. Tim Race, who runs the marvellous Mma Ramotswe Literary Tour, the only one of its kind in

*Now Bishop Trevor Mwamba of Botswana

Africa. His wife Claire, whose work has more than halved the transmission rate of HIV between mothers and babies in a clinical trial. American doctors confident that the AIDS tide is turning as more people see the very real benefits of retroviral drugs. Dr Moffat, relaxing for once, away from the hospital. Bujosi Olthogile, the Edinburgh-trained vice-chancellor of the country's university, who is pointing out to me how much Botswana owes to Scotland. Derek James, whom I'd last seen doing war-dances with the nursery class in his orphanage, surely one of the best-run in Africa.

The twelve young children, swaying and dancing as they sing for us in the Moffats' garden, are also orphans. Someone tells me they have made up all the words and music themselves. "Thank you, Mr Sandy," they sing. "Thank you for being with us. Please come back to see us, but thank you for just being here." And in the middle of this group of friends, under the Southern Cross, in the warmth of a Botswanan night, a kind-faced author in a kilt smiles back at them as he wipes a tear from his eye.

Zoë Wicomb

Toni Morrison and JM Coetzee are among her admirers, and students on the creative writing course she taught at Strathclyde University all sing her praises. Yet I've hardly ever met anyone less keen to be interviewed, and couldn't work out why such a confident, admired lecturer and such a highly-praised writer was so reluctant to talk about herself. The answer reaches right back into the dark heart of the apartheid society she left behind decades ago, but which still haunts her fiction.

O SAY that Zoë Wicomb doesn't enjoy interviews is like saying that four-year-old boys don't, as a rule, bounce happily into the dentist's chair and invite the attentions of syringe and drill. Why this should be so isn't immediately apparent – since Wicomb, South Africa-born but living in Glasgow for the last thirteen years, is a writer of rare brilliance. On the cover of her latest book, the Nobel laureate Toni Morrison and the double Booker winner JM Coetzee compete to eulogise her work. She's formidably intelligent: "A mind like a steel trap", says the head of the Scottish Arts Council's literature department, "one of the brightest people you could meet." She is, according to her students at Strathclyde University, where Wicomb holds a professorship, a peerless and inspiring teacher. Yet the chances are that you won't have heard of her, because this is the first British newspaper interview she has ever given. For the thirty years she's lived in Britain, that's the way she's liked it, and to be honest, it probably still is.

Wicomb's new novel, *Playing in the Light*, is one of the most convincing I've read all year. If she's going for the title of Scotland's greatest unknown novelist, it's hers on a plate. *Playing in the Light* opens with a successful, white, Cape Town businesswoman visiting her father, a retired traffic policeman. Apartheid has ended, the Rainbow Nation has been born, and at the travel agency she runs, Marion Campbell is slowly making adjustments. To her father John, an unreconstructed Afrikaner, the country he once served proudly as a reservist is going to the dogs, blarry kaffirs dragging it further into anarchy, further from the idyllic past when they knew their place. At first, you might think that's all the story is going to be, and Wicomb's characterisation is so compellingly acute that this would be enough. It would be a story of quiet accommodations, of the slow tensions of change: Marion relaxing in her luxurious apartment, looking out over the beach that she has long since learnt not to walk on at night; Brenda Mackay, the travel agency's first black employee, calmly challenging old assumptions; John Campbell drinking whisky, dreaming of golden childhood summers on the veldt. In lives such as these, the abstract nouns of the Truth and Reconciliation Committee are made flesh. But Wicomb, subtly seeding her story with symbols, allusions and half-buried memories, goes deeper. As she gets under the skin of her two main characters, she uncovers something else altogether. Another skin, and a skin of a different colour too.

They called them "play-whites", people like John Campbell and his wife Helen. If apartheid had been absolutely impermeable; if officialdom were impervious to bribery; if rules were incapable of being bent, they would have been categorised as "coloured" from birth, and through every single year of their lives. Opportunities – to get on in life, or to get out of South Africa – were only available to whites. So among some families who were classed as coloured, but who could pass for white, sacrifices were made so they could do just that. And what sacrifices! For the Campbells, it meant turning their lives inside out. They couldn't be seen with their darker-skinned relatives, so family life became a sequence of absences, from empty pews at weddings to missing mourners at funerals. The family home had to be abandoned, and sisters and brothers renounced. Grandparents could only come and visit if they pretended to be – and dressed as – servants. Surnames had to be changed; ancestors' photographs painted over; lips and noses thinned; thick-soled feet scraped tender. And all the time, there was a fear of exposure: of what a casual incriminating word, or an unnerving remembrance of love, or a racially inappropriate memory, could lead to. There would be no room for dreams, or not real ones, anyway: only vigilance and consistency, aliases and alibis, ready-prepared answers, and constant fear.

Would a second child come out white, like Marion had? Perhaps not, so no second child, and yet another absence for tension to fill, like air rushing into a vacuum, the pressure growing all the time, "*as if the very plaster was giving its all to prevent the house from exploding*". Wicomb pulls Marion from her sterile luxury flat, and the comforts of a life founded on apartheid, and pitches her into a journey through thickets of lacerating lies, back to her family's past. At the same time, this is a voyage into the new South Africa, where the old divisions have been constitutionally shrunk away, but where they still remain, like hidden cancers.

Wicomb was born in Namaqueland, a hot arid region on the southern fringes of the Namib desert, in 1948. The good life of white South Africa was a long way from this sparsely populated scrubland, and the nearest whites lived twenty miles away, in the town which also had the nearest shop – though, as coloureds, the Wicombs couldn't actually go in and shop there: they were served, instead, from a hatch round the side. Her Afrikaans-speaking parents wanted the best for their children: something more than the two local job options of working in the gypsum mine or becoming a domestic servant. Speaking English – as no-one did for two hundred miles around – wasn't an automatic free pass to a better life, but it was a better bet than anything else. Secondary school meant Cape Town, where she lived with her aunt. A school for coloureds, followed by a university for coloureds, where she learnt about such great non-coloureds as Chaucer, Johnson, Shakespeare and Hardy. And where, for the first time, Wicomb caught sight of "play-whites". "There was a family living across the road from us, and one day they just disappeared. Our neighbours said, 'They've left. They've turned white'. This happened all the time."

"It's an odd phenomenon, the play-whites," says Wicomb. "We don't even know how many of them there are. There's no discourse, nothing in the library, because officially they don't exist. Yet the truth of the matter, because of their history, is that many Afrikaners are mixed race. Even Verwoerd [the founder of apartheid] had a wife who looked African." Because skin colour is so variable, even within the same family, legal definitions of whiteness were absurdly tortuous. "A white person," the government decided in 1950, "is someone who in appearance obviously is or is generally accepted as a white person, but does not include a person who, although in appearance obviously a white person, is generally accepted as a coloured person." Mrs Verwoerd presumably counted as white not because she looked it but because enough people could agree that she was. "The weird thing," says Wicomb, "was that there was this legislation for racial purity at the same time as the whites were tacitly boosting their own numbers by allowing some people to cross over." The blurred edges of all racial groups contain their own potential tragedies. "The newspapers were always full of stories about abandoned children found tied up or living under the bed because their families were ashamed of them on account of the colour of their skin," says Wicomb. "On the other hand, when I was at school, I remember kids in my class boasting about the members of their family who had 'turned white'." And by the same token, given the coloureds' formal rights under apartheid to live in South Africa, some blacks were just as keen to recategorise themselves as coloured.

This is the first time that the history of "play-whites" has been approached in South African literary fiction. So why, with such an intriguing subject, so commandingly handled; with Toni Morrison praising her "seductive, brilliant, precious talent" on her book's cover; with former pupils lining up to credit her for helping them become published writers – just why is Wicomb, in the words of one, "the most self-effacing writer I've ever met"? She isn't, she insists, a real writer: she doesn't think of herself as one. Apart from sabbaticals and holidays, she hardly writes at all, and when she does, it's "torture, painfully slow". Her university work is different: that's what pays the bills, that's where she finds it easy to talk about literature, that's where she studies nothing but the very best, like Coetzee. And she sighs, just at the thought of his so-beautifully constructed sentences, beside which her own.... Her voice tails off. And because the teaching, rather than the writing, is the priority in her life, she deliberately chooses to be published by small presses, free from interfering editors demanding rewrites on a whim, and from publicists drawing up an impossible round of interviews. The books, she says, will find their own way without her.

She doesn't like talking about her own life too much, but switch to South African history or the politics of race, and it's a different matter. History played a cruel trick on her, she says: the anti-apartheid resistance movement was weak in the late Sixties, when she was a student, and she left the country two years before Steve Biko's black consciousness movement took hold on the campuses. "I was hot-headed, impatient, I just wanted to leave the whole oppressiveness of my own culture far behind." In exile in London, a shy girl surprised at hearing herself speak in public, she took up the fight against race hate. Sometimes it seemed surprisingly close at hand: Scotland, she noted on arrival in 1989, seemed a much more racist country than England (it's no accident that nearly all of the characters in her novel have Scottish surnames). Yet even after all these years, she remains unable to shake off her birth country's hold. "I have a ghost existence here: my whole intellectual and emotional life is in South Africa."

But while that may be understandable, the blanket of self-effacement with which she talks about her writing still seems to need some explaining. What it all boils down to, she finally says, is this: "I'm very, very contrary. And I want to be in control, which is what informs my attitude to publishing, editing, being interviewed. I set high standards too: as a reader, I don't read any poor novels, so I'm always aware of how much my own work falls flat by comparison. And perhaps it's because I grew up in South Africa, and it was easy there for people like me to grow up with a consciousness of inferiority." So still it lingers, the shadow of a political system so barbarous and absurd that it becomes increasingly hard to imagine. Read this novel, so nuanced, so precise, and so much better than its author can bring herself to admit, and it's back, rivetingly captured in all its soul-shrivelling force.

P.S. - **Playing in the Light** by Zoë Wicomb is available in paperback from The New Press. Her previous novel, **David's Story,** and the short story cycle **You Can't Get Lost in Cape Town** are both published by The Feminist Press.

David Mitchell

His novel 'Cloud Atlas' was still a month away from publication in February 2004 when I went to West Cork to visit its author, but already the hype about it was building. In person, he is as modest and unassuming as his books are multi-layered and genre-juggling, though as he points out, their 'secret architecture' depends on coincidence and correspondences. On the way back home, I inadvertently discovered how one such coincidence helped him find his way into his next novel.

LACK OF imagination is never going to be David Mitchell's problem. His first novel, the award-winning *Ghostwritten*, raced through the minds of a terrorist planting nerve gas in the Tokyo underground, a counter-revolutionary Mongolian monk, a late-night New York DJ, a redundant English spy, a ghost, and an Irish physicist on the run. All that, far more, and an apocalypse too. In *number9dream*, shortlisted for the 2002 Man Booker Prize, a Japanese student's search for his father breaks into scenes of Yakuza gang violence, Second World War suicide missions, a dreamy romance and yes, another – slightly smaller – apocalypse. His latest novel, *Cloud Atlas*, which his publishers are already ramping up as a Man Booker favourite, brings the world to an end even earlier than usual, halfway through the novel. Already, though, the reader has been pulled through a whole series of stories: an American voyager across the Pacific in the mid-nineteenth century, a gay amanuensis to an elderly composer living in Belgium in the 1930s, a journalist on the trail of skullduggery in the American nuclear power industry, a black farce about a London publisher, and a slave-class rebellion in a dystopic brave new world.

From all of this, you might expect to find a certain type of writer answering the door when you call at his home. The kind whose imagination slips the leash uncontrollably, slavering for Armageddon. Posters of exploding supernovae on the walls, the complete *Star Trek* collection on the DVD rack, shoot-'em-up gang-ster games on the PS2, bookshelves stocked with the arcane and the frankly unreadable, and a ready supply of green ink for writing in. A beard, of course; a degree in engineering, naturally. Instead of which, you head down to the end of a lane in the West Cork town of Clonakilty, find a whitewashed holiday cottage looking across to the hills sloping down to the sea, and meet David Mitchell.

He's 35, and has lived in Clonakilty for four months with his Japanese wife Keiko. They met in 1997, in the middle of the eight years he spent in Japan as an English teacher. Their eighteen-month-old daughter Hana is one of the most beautiful toddlers I have seen. Mitchell himself is friendly, helpful, and without any detectable hint of writerly ego. A mutual friend who broke the news to him that he was on the Man Booker shortlist told me that his only reaction was to say "Great!" before, without a beat, switching the conversation back to her, how she'd been keeping, and so on. A modest man, in other words, with a lot to be immodest about. No trace of any green ink, real or metaphorical, either. The Mitchell imagination may be wide-ranging, but the manacles he puts on it are impressive. His writing might explode into the most dazzling pyrotechnics, but they are deliberately controlled, defiantly post-modern, big bangs. So although *Ghostwritten* snaked across conti-nents and through a dazzling array of minds, the stories were always on a tight, interlinking string. *number9dream* performs similar switchbacks across time and place, but what really drove it was Mitchell's need to write within a variety of self-imposed limitations: the first story, about the Japanese Aum terrorist was really about the abnegation of imagination, the second about memory, and other narrative threads took the form of nightmare, journals, metaphysi-cal riddles, cyberspace and finally, good old-fashioned romance.

And so to *Cloud Atlas*. Here the limitation – the "secret archi-tecture", Mitchell calls it – isn't as complex as it was when he planned the novel. Originally, he wanted to tell nine separate stories, all interconnected: three in the past, three in the present and three in the future. In the final version, which is already a fairly bulky book, there are only two of each. This structural complexity makes *Cloud Atlas* difficult to summarise. The journals of an American travelling across the Pacific in the nineteenth century are found and sold in the 1930s by Robert Frobisher, a composer who writes the *Cloud Atlas Sextet*, while working for a Delius-like figure in Belgium and corresponding with a man who was his gay lover at university. Fifty years later, in another chapter and another genre, Frobisher's correspondent is a scientist whom investigative journalist Louisa Rey is trying to persuade to blow the whistle on a dangerous nuclear power project in California. By now we are deep in metafictional thriller territory: in the next chapter, this story turns out to be a manuscript submitted to a down-at-heel English publisher by its author. Both the publisher and the author, one Lesley V Hush, have already had bit-parts in *Ghostwritten*: this web of interconnectedness spreads not only within the book, but across Mitchell's *oeuvre*. The Louisa Rey mystery chapter is unabashed pulp fiction – the hardest part to write, Mitchell says, as the genre almost demands unoriginality. Yet part of him is even now considering writing an airport thriller under the name of Lesley V Hush. "I'm hankering to write a second Louisa Rey mystery and publish it as a sort of Patricia Cornwell novel with Hush's name in raised embossed letters. I'd like to call it *Bougainvillea* and see it on the shelves in Tesco." He laughs, but I think he's serious.

As far as Mitchell's own secret architecture is concerned, perhaps the first stop should be the thesis he did for his post-graduate degree in comparative literature: "Levels of Reality in the Post-Modern Novel". "What a self-aggrandising title," he winces, but the subject of fictions within fiction, where one has clear consequences for the other (as in the play-within-a-play in *Hamlet*), clearly still informs his work. For the science fiction strand in *Cloud Atlas*, the roots go further back. "The earliest books to make an impact on me are all part of that British end-of-the-world tradition in science fiction. JG Ballard, say, or John Wyndham's *The Chrysalids*: that's a fantastic piece of writing that would stand up even now and should be up there with *Brave New World*. There was something about growing up in Britain during the Cold War and those books spoke to it. They had a strong impact on me. I used to worry that when it started raining it would never stop. I would wonder, what if it didn't? What if the trucks stopped delivering to the supermarkets and people started scrambling for food? I spoke to some Italians and Dutch people recently about how we used to worry about the Third World War, and it seemed as if on the Continent they never did. But me and my mates at school, we did worry about it, and I don't think it ever quite goes away."

Mitchell grew up by the vast sands of Southport, in Lancashire, and moved to rural Worcestershire, in the shadow of the Malvern Hills, when he was eight. It was, he says, an uncomplicated, happy childhood. "My parents were both artists, and there was always an amount of cartridge paper around, the size of a Sunday newspaper. I'd spend hours and days and weeks drawing the kind of maps you get at the end of Tolkien's *Return of the King*. I'd draw islands and continents and people, and I suppose that's a kind of narrative right there, because already you're talking about wars or journeys. It's the same part of my head then that I use now when I work." But it's Mitchell's love of language that separates him from other tricksy postmodernists, and that gives *Cloud Atlas* its astonishing breadth. From the Herman Melville-influenced archaic language of the opening chapter to the decomposing, post-apocalyptic language of the Pacific islanders at the book's centre, his words take us inside the heads of a dizzying variety of protagonists, across centuries and continents. Frobisher writes in a suicide note that, now he has completed his *Cloud Atlas Sextet*, he no longer feels a need to live. "*I may be a spent firework, but at least I've been a firework,*" he writes. That's exactly what the novel is: a starburst of dreams – showy maybe, but as extravagant as the last rocket in a firework display.

Let's stick with that analogy for a moment. If you set fire to a tray of gunpowder, it burns with a hiss rather than a bang: it's only when you put it in a container that it soars and explodes. So it is with Mitchell, the literary firework-maker in Clonakilty: the more limits he imposes on his writing, the bigger the bang. "It's the challenges you set yourself, the difficulties, the frames, the straitjackets, that force writing to be ingenious. With historical fiction, that constraint is the language: you've got to get it absolutely right, and it can be incredibly time-consuming. The first ninety pages of the book, set in the nineteenth century, took me about a year and a half. But you've got to get the authenticity right to establish that magic, just the same way that I've got to make exactly the right noises if I can get Hana, who's learning to speak, to bring something in from the next room."

The interconnectedness of the stories in *Cloud Atlas* is another part of Mitchell's liberating straitjacket. In the novel, not only is each thread a variation on the theme of individuals being preyed upon – by the tribe, by other individuals, by big business and so on – but innumerable other links are woven between them. Several of the characters have, for example, a comet-shaped birthmark, as if to suggest that they might in fact be the same narrator, although Mitchell doesn't push that suggestion too far. All of which makes his choice of subject for the next novel completely surprising. He shows me the notebooks on which he plans out his books and there is a drawing, from an aerial perspective, of ten back gardens on a suburban street, with the plants in them and the kind of fences or hedges between them clearly marked. "I'm trying to remember, in trainspotterish detail, everything about the world as I saw it in 1982: the visceral thrill of the Falklands and its sad victory, the precise schoolboy slang that we used, maybe just for six months. And that picture is about what we used to do in the summer nights: creeping through our neighbours' back gardens, trying to get the length of the street without being noticed."

The day after my interview with Mitchell, I sat next to children's author Keith Gray on a train journey from Glasgow to Edinburgh. We got to talking about writers who were more successful in one country than their own, and he told me that his first book, *Creepers* – which involved the very children's game Mitchell described – was a best-seller in Japan, despite being out of print here. Last year, Gray was on Radio 4, talking about how childhood had changed since the days of Enid Blyton, and he mentioned the game of creeping unnoticed across his neighbours' back gardens. Over in Clonakilty, David Mitchell was listening to the radio while cooking. He didn't catch Gray's name, just that story of children creeping through their neighbours' back gardens on summer nights. Yes, he thought, that's what we used to do too, that summer of '82, and as he started to think of what else he did, the idea of a book began to form....

The string of coincidences amazes him: that he'd shown me the one page about that story, that I'd accidentally met the one man in the world who'd inadvertently been its inspiration. "Couldn't make it up, eh?" he laughs. And when the modern master of the interconnected novel says that, you have to agree that, no, probably no-one could.

P.S. - *Following this interview,* **Cloud Atlas** *was shortlisted for the 2004 Man Booker Prize. The "next novel" referred to turned out to be the amazing* **Black Swan Green**, *published in 2006. In 2007, David Mitchell was listed as one of Time Magazine's 100 most influential people in the world. All of David Mitchell's fiction is available in paperback from Sceptre. I'm also delighted to report that, since this piece was first published, Keith Gray's* **Creepers** *has gone back into print, and is available in paperback.*

JG Ballard

The few people lucky enough to interview JG Ballard tend to write about the oddity of finding the owner of such a maverick mind living in a Shepperton semi. That's where I met him in January 2008, to talk about his auto-biography. He was seriously ill with prostate cancer and clearly hated the attentions of my photographer's flash, wincing slightly each time it went off. Generously, though, he poured out a bottle of Chablis for us. We wished him good health.

SK WILL SELF about the man sitting across the table from me and he'd say he is the most important writer in Britain. Ask John Sutherland, twice chair of the Booker judges, and he'd say the same. Ask the publisher's reader who first ran her eye over the manuscript for *Crash* and she'd say he "is beyond psychiatric help".

JG Ballard and I are in the unkempt living room of a Shepperton semi; his home for nearly fifty years. A grey behemoth of an IBM electric typewriter is on the table between us, covered with a grubby dust jacket. It is entirely probable that more visionary dystopias have been battered out of that machine than any other one like it. So have two of the most searingly honest autobiographies of the last few decades: the one fictionalised in *Empire of the Sun* and, now, the book he says will be his last: his stoical, unpretentious, clear-sighted and fascinating memoir, *Miracles of Life.* If you're looking for keys to nearly all of Ballard's disturbingly prescient dystopias – worlds half-drowned by apocalyptic climate change, shopping malls under attack by empty-headed consumerists, middle classes trashing the Tate and marching on the BBC, high-rise residents turning on each other like starved lab rats – they're all here, as clearly explanatory as notes for a retrospective exhibition. For years, he says, he resisted the idea that his fiction was mainly rooted in the violence and societal breakdown he saw as a boy growing up in pre-war Shanghai, and particularly the three years he spent in a Japanese internment camp. Now, aged 77 and battling advanced prostate cancer, he's changed his mind.

The city of his childhood was so full of magical and miserable memories, he says, that "I think a large part of my fiction has been an attempt to evoke it by means other than memory". Even before the Japanese came, death was daily visible: each morning the street cleaners would shovel up the corpses of hundreds of destitute Chinese who had died on its cold pavements during the night. Those marginally richer, but still too poor to afford coffins, would float their loved ones' bodies, decked out with paper flowers, on to sewage streams. Those richer still would bury corpses in small piles of earth that were often washed away when the heavy rains came, leaving the bodies exposed. At 31 Acacia Drive, a surreally Surrey stockbroker mansion in Shanghai's plushest suburb, the young Ballard was cocooned by privilege. His mother, once voted the city's best-dressed woman, would while away her time over cards and cocktails at the Country Club. His businessman father earned enough to support a lavish lifestyle: there were ten Chinese servants, all unnamed, in the annexe at the back of the house – itself twice as big as his Shepperton semi – and a chauffeured Buick in the drive. In a city of unregulated capitalism, the Ballards were near the top of the heap.

Even when he was six, though, he realised something was wrong. One winter's day, from the back of the Buick, he noticed a beggar by the gates of the drive to the house. The old man rattled a tobacco tin at passers-by, but no-one gave him any change. Each day, he was there, starving, slowly dying in the snow. "Imagine that here," says Ballard, pointing out towards the front window, past a yucca plant that sprawls across the table between us like an unravelled wickerwork elephant's trunk, a few desperate green tips touching the lace curtains. "Right now, I mean. Someone dying just out there, over five days, and nobody in here doing a thing to help.

What's the point of that?" I look out through the dusty lace at a battered Vauxhall, parked behind a wheelie bin in the overgrown front garden. A few children shuffle by, laughing, on their way home from school. The next year – 1937 – the Japanese invaded. He saw bayoneted Chinese corpses in the streets, but the westerners' dinner parties went blithely on. "Most of the Europeans, adults and children, were completely indifferent to the horrors going on daily on the streets of the city. They just took it in their stride. There was nothing they could do, they told themselves, just as my mother told me there was no point in helping that beggar outside our drive because if we did give him anything, the next day there'd be whole crowds of beggars all expecting the same. So they just switched off their emotional responses. I for some reason didn't. I don't know why. Maybe because I was already telling stories to myself. And if you're doing that, you've got to know what the point of it all is."

The Japanese were the key. He could see that – which is why, unlike every other western child he met in Shanghai, he wanted to befriend their soldiers. Even without hindsight, he could already sense that his parents' world was doomed, their confidence in the British empire misplaced. His world's bedrock was already starting to shift, to become illusory. When he was twelve, and his family was interned, it would slip away completely.

He loved Lunghua camp. Well, "love" is the wrong word, because it was psychologically scarring, though it didn't seem like that at the time. But he didn't mind eating the weevils that came with the rice. He even developed a taste for a particular brand of cattle feed. His parents, once aloof and uninterested, were now living in the same room as him and his young sister. He liked that feeling of closeness: still does, which is why he and his own three children never moved from that small Shepperton semi, even when the film money from *Empire of the Sun* (1987) and *Crash* (1996) started rolling in. Another thing about the camp: he made more friends more easily than at any time in his life since – American sailors, flirtatious teenage girls, rogues, academics, ex-cons, all with plenty of time to talk.

At this point, it's easy enough to look back at Ballard's fiction and start to join the dots. All those images of half-empty or drained swimming pools – motifs for abandoned certainties – date right back to the first ones he saw, walking back to Acacia Drive after the end of internment. All those gated and embattled communities (*Super-Cannes*, *High-Rise*, etc.) are surely related to the besieged values of Acacia Drive, or to Lunghua camp itself. And as for Ballard's deliciously subversive imagination – well, what else would you expect from someone who, as a teenage internee, found enjoyment in privation, felt estrangement from his parents, and itched to fraternise with the Japanese enemy? Yet it's still years before Ballard becomes a writer, years more before he latches on to science fiction, discovers surrealism and Freud, and melds them into a new kind of writing form: exploring inner space rather than outer space, the "visionary present" rather than the escapist future. It's also too glib an explanation: those were real, dying people he saw. In fact, England, as much as China, made him the great maverick writer he is. "England, not Britain," he adds. "When I came back, I hated England."

This was 1946. The Mother Country looked every bit as battered, blown-apart, grey and beaten as it did to so many of those first West Indian immigrants, who walked down the gangplank of the Windrush only a year later. "England was living in a state of real denial about its identity. It had a total delusion about itself. I was brought up in Shanghai with all these English myths – *Just William* books, *Peter Pan*, all that – this vision of England as basically Knightsbridge and South Kensington with a bit of pleasant countryside thrown in, where everyone was essentially middle class. The only place it could turn was the past; all that flummery and mummery about the royal family, the class system still in place. In many ways we'd lost the war: we certainly didn't gain anything from it." He loathed his grandparents in West Bromwich, loathed the Black Country ("some of the worst housing in western Europe, with often barely literate people bombed out of their homes with nothing to look forward to but Hollywood films"), loathed the hidebound traditionalists he met at Cambridge, where he briefly studied medicine. And though history now looks back to Attlee's great socialist reforming government of 1945, though change was in the air, that is emphatically not, he says, what it felt like at the time.

The first two years at Cambridge, learning how to dissect bodies, fascinated him ("I was trying to understand what death really is"), but the rest of the course didn't – so he quit. He tried studying English, being a Covent Garden porter, selling encyclopaedias, then went on an RAF officer training course in Canada that turned out nuclear bomber pilots. It didn't last – though at one windswept air force base in the Rockies, he did at least discover science fiction. He told his parents he wanted to be a writer. "They must have despaired of you," I say. He nods sadly. "Being a serial drop-out and all." He demurs: that sounds far too hippyish for him. "Finding your own career path was just a lot harder then." But here's the point: if Ballard had fitted in, he wouldn't have been a writer. If he had gone to California, he'd have had all the modernity he craved, found himself living in a country that was everything he wanted Britain to be – and probably not written a word. If he'd never seen the madness, death and magic of Shanghai at an impressionable age – and then, crucially, been unable to return there after the Communist revolution – he surely wouldn't have felt the deracination that drove his imagination, that pushed him further towards surrealism, the avant garde, and everything that now makes up the adjective "Ballardian": that feeling of a modernity always on an uneasy tilt, always on the brink of extinction, always about to be wiped out by some new kind of barbarism; the feeling that middle-class solidities – even in Shepperton – still cannot be trusted.

He's 77 now, and cancer is tightening its hold on his body, moving into his spine and ribs. Yet there's no hint of self-pity about him, either in person or in his final book. Is this stoicism in the face of his own death yet another effect of having seen too much death too early in his own life? "To some extent, that neutralises your feelings," he says. "Yet on the other hand it's corrupting. You're recruited into death's world by witnessing too much of it. It can make you very cold and can strip away ideals and illusions." I think straight away of his short story "The Dead Time", in which a man charged with driving away corpses for burial after the liberation of the internment camps realises that he himself has already subtly passed over into the world of the dead.

Before he tires, I ask him one final question. In my mind, I call it the "Stephen Fry question" after an interview I saw in which, talking about his manic depression, he was asked whether he would prefer to have lived a life with or without that condition. With Ballard, who is more genial and avuncular than bipolar, the question frames itself differently, but is essentially the same: would he have preferred an ordinary life? He looks across at me, this kind, elderly man whom I shall never meet again. "No. Because what's the alternative? Being brought up here in Shepperton-on-Thames or some godawful suburb of Swindon? No. I'm glad I was born in Shanghai, glad I saw the city at its height, glad I went through the war and that I survived. It was such an extraordinary experience – damaging too, because it takes away your ideals, and you no longer trust your parents because you're watching them under stress. But it enriched my life."

P.S. - At the time of writing, **Miracles of Life** is available in hardback from Fourth Estate. Ballard's most recent novel **Kingdom Come** (2006) is also published by Fourth Estate, in paperback, and a two-volume edition of his **Complete Short Stories** is published by Flamingo.

JG Ballard has published a total of 35 books, and all the other titles mentioned in this interview are available in paperback. For further information on JG Ballard, and links to the huge variety of writers he has inspired, the website www.jgballard.com is a good source.

Yiyun Li

She was in San Francisco and couldn't travel, for fear of not being allowed back into the United States, so that's why this interview with the Chinese short story writer Yiyun Li is the only one here to have been conducted by telephone. Face-to-face interviews are invariably more nuanced and revealing, but Li's is such an amazing story — and such an incredible talent — that on this occasion it didn't seem to matter. This was her first British interview, in February 2006.

HE FIRST time Yiyun Li saw a group of prisoners on their way to execution, she was five. There were three men and a woman, their hands bound with ropes, and they shuffled on to a makeshift stage in a field in suburban Beijing. An officer raised his fist, shouting: "Death to the counter-revolutionary hooligans!" And the five-year-old Li was happy to see them go, because a world free of hooligans, of those who would dare to harm China's socialist paradise, was clearly a better place.

In *A Thousand Years of Good Prayers* — winner of the inaugural Frank O'Connor prize, the world's most lucrative award for a collection of short stories — Yiyun Li explores more than just the kinds of things those counter-revolutionary hooligans might have done. Hers are stories of immense brilliance and subtlety, skewering the bitter realities of everyday life; not only under Mao, but also under his successors' great leap forward into bare-knuckle capitalism. In the future, historians will look back on China's first steps towards superpower status as the most important economic transformation since the Industrial Revolution. To understand what those changes meant to ordinary Chinese people at the time, they will read Li's stories of old men meeting for tea in the cafés outside the nascent stock markets; young men dreaming of a new life in the US, able to send back money to their relatives; old women left without a pension by the collapse of state factories, or finding jobs as maids at the country's first private schools. They'll be raked over too by social historians charting attitudinal change: when the young first began kissing in public without fear, when women dared to disagree directly with their menfolk, when students saw their first American film.

But that's not the only reason Yiyun Li is worth reading. Like her favourite writer, William Trevor, she perfectly captures nuances of thought and action in her stories, dropping the reader into immediately believable worlds. She has been published in the *New Yorker* and the *Paris Review*, and won a shoal of literary awards. "She is," Salman Rushdie points out, "the real thing." She's also a mere 33 years old and – most astonishingly of all – only started writing in English six years ago. Despite all that, any day now an envelope could drop through her letter box in Oakland, California, informing her that her second appeal for a green card has been turned down. If she is declared an illegal immigrant, she could be put on a plane straight back to China, along with her husband and two young sons. Her perilous legal status in the US was underlined last October when she was unable to pick up her prize in Cork: she didn't dare attend the ceremony in case she was refused re-entry to the States. In theory, the US does allow foreign artists of "extraordinary ability" to live there; in practice, this is interpreted impossibly narrowly. Being the world's contemporary Chekhov, its modern Maupassant, does not, it seems, count for much. If Li had carried on with her post-graduate studies in immunology at Iowa university, she would herself be immune: the US has no problem admitting scientists working "for the national interest", and the majority of Li's former Beijing classmates are already working legally in the US under precisely those terms. Or, if she wrote crude anti-communist propaganda instead of wonderfully humane short stories, she would automatically qualify for an officially sanctioned, hassle-free existence in the US as a political dissident. The problem – or the irony – is that Li is not a dissident. She has lived in the US for the last ten years, but won't turn her back on China. Her parents still live there, and one day she'd like to go and see them.

Will it ever happen? "I don't know," she says. "Even though I refuse to allow my book to be translated into Chinese, I don't know how it will be accepted in China. But I am a Chinese citizen, and if I go back there and they do something to me, no-one will ever know. Even naturalised Americans have been back and arrested for all kinds of ridiculous reasons. There's always this worry for Chinese intellectuals overseas: it's not always safe for us to go back."

As to why that should be, let's consider "Son", one of the stories in the collection, about a Chinese software engineer working in America who goes back, after ten years, to Beijing. His mother, a former party member, has become a Christian after her husband's death, and has for years been trying to marry him off. He's never told her that he is gay. So he wanders into an internet café and tries to log on to a few gay chat rooms before he realises that the internet police have blanked them all out. After arguing with his mother about her new-found faith, he accompanies her to church. He doesn't go in, and when his mother tries to bribe some beggar children to attend the service with her, he gives them twice the money not to. He sits in a Starbucks across the road, from where he hears an accident outside: there are so many these days, he notes, because corruption has grown so endemic that the newly-rich get other people to take their driving tests for them. And the beggar-children, who have been run down – well, there's an inexhaustible supply of them too.

There, within that one story, is both a metaphor for Li's plight (Americana on the Starbucks side of the street, Chinese tradition on the other, an accident in the middle) and an example of why the Chinese authorities would dislike her fiction. To them, "Son" – with its child beggars, Christianity, censorship, corruption – would read like an indictment of the regime. To us, these are almost incidentals. Like its companion piece, the title story, in which a Chinese girl in America is visited by her ageing father, it's really about love: "*It takes 3,000 years of prayers to place your head side by side with your loved one's on the pillow. For father and daughter? A thousand years maybe.*" Li must know, deep down, that it would be asking too much of the authorities to expect them to recognise "Son" as, at heart, a beautifully constructed tale about the love between parent and child. They have a catch-all phrase for those who say the regime isn't the best of all possible worlds. They call them "counter-revolutionary hooligans", and she's known what can happen to people like that ever since she was five.

When, I ask, did she lose her child's faith in the regime? I thought I could guess the answer: Tiananmen Square happened when she was a sixteen, a pupil at an elite school, fifteen minutes' cycle ride from the square. Her school only admitted the brightest and best – surely the most likely to be enthused by the possibilities of democracy. But her discontent had other roots too. "When I was twelve or thirteen, I never thought for a moment that we didn't live in heaven. We were taught to look up to our teachers because in some way they represented the state, yet a couple of them were, I now realise, child molesters. With one of them, I just thought he liked me a lot, but he touched me inappropriately – not just me but other girls too." Even before then, there had been seeds of doubt. At Beijing's Friendship Hotel, where foreigners lived in a luxury denied to local Chinese, she'd seen a couple of white children riding around on tiny bikes with stabilisers. This small awareness of inequality, of envy, combined with family secrets to feed her disaffection – and the family had no bigger secret than that her grandfather and two of her mother's uncles had fought on the "wrong" side in the civil war between the nationalists and communists. In 1949, after the nationalists' defeat, one officer uncle had fled, with his shattered army, to Taiwan. They didn't hear from him for another forty years. "My parents would say, don't ever talk about him. We were trained early on to keep secrets." All the same, by the time she was thirteen, there were distinct signs of a new openness. "Between 1985 and 1987, there was a huge wave of translating western philosophers. I got to read a lot of them – Sartre, Camus, Rousseau – and it was a fundamental part of my education," she says.

When the Tiananmen Square demonstrations broke out, Li realised she was witnessing a key moment in Chinese history, yet she was too young to participate. After school, she and her friends would read the posters on the college walls, and visit the demonstrators. She was particularly moved by a group of middle-aged men standing quietly by the roadside. The placards round their necks read: "We have knelt down all our life. This is our opportunity to stand up as human beings." Her parents told her not to be so idealistic, that troops would soon be ordered to kill the students. After it happened, her school was closed for a week. A friend who had been in the square on the night the tanks moved in told her how the demonstrators had been crushed in their tents. A month later, the police took him away. No-one knew who could be trusted. Officially, there'd been no massacre. That's what the television news had said on the night it happened, but all Li's friends knew someone who'd been killed. Along with all her classmates, she had to sign up for a year of political re-education in the army before being allowed to study at Beijing University. One day, she forgot her mother's injunction – "Imagine a zipper on your mouth. Zip it up tight" – and told her squad the real story about Tiananmen Square. Although the squad leader reported her, his superior officer decided to take no action.

Only in America did the fetters on her thought start to fall away. As she learnt to write in a foreign language, she began to express herself more freely – not just about politics, but about everything else too. At last, she didn't have any secrets to keep, whether about her mother's counter-revolutionary uncles, or the students who died in 1989. In English she could start afresh, with a more direct way of talking and thinking. As the Chinese-American protagonist tells her father in the story "Baba": "...*if you grew up in a language that you never used to express your feelings, it would be easier to take up another language and talk more in the new language. It makes you a new person*". A new person, and a great writer. And if her old country and her new one don't realise that, their loss is enormous.

P.S. - *A Thousand Years of Good Prayers has now won four major prizes, including the 2006 Guardian First Book Award. It is available in paperback from Harper Perennial. In 2007, Yiyun Li was chosen as one of Granta's Best of Young American Novelists. At the time of writing, her eagerly anticipated first novel — currently untitled — is due to be published by Fourth Estate in August 2008. Yiyun Li has a website at www.yiyunli.com Her US visa problem, she tells me, has now been resolved.*

Tobias Wolff

"Zelig", I told American writer Tobias Wolff. "That's who you are." In Woody Allen's film of that name, he's a human cipher who inserts himself into key events of twentieth-century history. Already Wolff had joked that maybe it was him at Oxford who'd passed Bill Clinton that joint he didn't inhale. He'd told me about being at boarding school with Oliver Stone and watching Kennedy's broadcast with him during the Cuban missile crisis. Then he mentioned the time he was on the fringes of another American political cataclysm . . .

I F EVER he needed it, it would look good on the CV. The *Washington Post*: summer of Watergate. Tobias Wolff was only a junior reporter on the obituaries desk and he hated the job. He had been picked for it over his flat-mate, and it was slowly poisoning their friendship. Each day, for six months, there would be a small knot of dread inside him when he turned up to work in a vast room, big as a football pitch, which they'd made by smashing up all the old wood-and-frosted glass partitions. Those would have suited him just fine. Anything to stop editor Ben Bradlee constantly checking that the young recruit was pulling his weight. Even now, Wolff still can't work when anybody else is watching. Most of the senior reporters were much too stiff to like, but Carl Bernstein was different. Carl was red-hot that summer. He couldn't believe what was happening, how every time they'd turn over a stone, there'd be ten more bugs scurrying away. You'd feel left out of all that excitement, toiling away on obituaries, but Carl would somehow share it with everybody. Even with the death desk.

By this time, though, Wolff is already looking for a way out of journalism. He's slacking at his job, doesn't check the obvious, knows that he'd really much rather be a writer. That's what he'd been telling everybody at Oxford the previous year and, as he'd since got a First in English, maybe some of them were starting to believe him. He still has a British friend from his dreaming spires days who remembers that there were two American students who annoyed him: one for boasting that he was going to be president, the other for saying that he was going to be this great writer. Odd, that. It's exactly the way things turned out.

One slow news day on the *Washington Post*, for a joke, someone phones through an obituary for a man who is not yet dead. Wolff doesn't bother ringing the undertaker to check. But as he gets bawled out by his editor, maybe the left part of his brain is already flashing a message to the right: There's a story here. One day.

In person, Wolff is uncannily like his prose: lean, muscled, unfooled. There's no drenching ego; no effete, writerly flourishes. As he talks about his latest book of short stories – which leads off with an imaginative spin on the obituarist's tale – the impression is of the writer as craftsman, planing away pointless connecting phrases, holding back the metaphors until they really count, polishing paragraphs diamond-bright. Much of his work, he says, depends on creative rewriting. He quotes the example of Chekhov's short story "Lady With Pet Dog". "In the first draft Gourov comes out of his club in Moscow and meets a friend standing outside. Out of the blue, Gourov says: 'I met the most remarkable woman in Yalta last summer.' His friend says: 'Oh really?' and they get to talking about her. Later, Gourov says something about the sturgeon being a bit off. 'Yes, it was,' says his friend. In Chekhov's second draft, he still has Gourov say: 'I met the most remarkable woman in Yalta last summer.' But then he makes his friend say: 'You're right, the sturgeon was a little off tonight.'

"That's genius," says Tobias Wolff. "None of the other stuff was vital, and by cutting it, Chekhov just underlines Gourov's loneliness: he can't even talk to a friend about this woman who haunts him, he knows he has to see her again himself. That's the kind of editing I want to do on my stories, to be that open to radical change. It gives the story wings."

He's lived in Syracuse for seventeen years: married with three children, secure, content. But when he thinks of home, he still imagines driving into the dark, wooded mountains north of Seattle, the journey he describes at the end of his unforgettable childhood memoir, *This Boy's Life*. His friend Chuck, a seventeen-year-old alcoholic, is at the wheel, and Wolff is looking wistfully at the world he is about to leave, his wallet bulging with dollar bills from pawning the guns he stole from his stepfather for the great escape. It's an unpropitious start to adulthood, or it would have been, had he not already forged the recommendations that got him into a Princeton feeder school out east. Before that, the usual litany of juvenile delinquency – vandalising the school, shoplifting, taking the brakes off cars parked on steep streets and watching them crash – seemed to have marked out a bleaker future. The small, company-owned village of Chinook, where he lived with his mother and his hated redneck stepfather, held out few possibilities. There was seasonal logging work, and there were welfare cheques through the long, cold winters. There was really nothing else – unless you counted drinking.

Years later, when they were teaching together in Vermont, his friend Raymond Carver would argue with him that the American Dream was a sham: once a place like Chinook had you in its grimy embrace, there was no escape. Wolff would say there was, that you just had to reinvent yourself; discover a pose. That's what he was doing, even as a child, when he changed his name to Jack (after Jack London) and dreamed of a life on the wild frontier. That's what he was doing when he picked out Vance Packard's *The Status Seekers*, the ultimate guide to effective American social climbing, changed his name to Tobias von Ansell-Wolff III, and started applying for scholarships to posh schools. That's what he was doing when he went to Vietnam, even if this time he didn't bother trying to change his name to Hemingway.

In 1990, he went back to Chinook with the Scottish film director Michael Caton-Jones, for the filming of *This Boy's Life* (starring Robert De Niro as his stepfather, Ellen Barkin as his mother and Leonardo Di Caprio as the teenage Wolff), and met some of his friends from the old days. If Carver had been right, they would still all be stuck in dead-end jobs, but they weren't. "We'd been walking the razor's edge, but we all got lucky. There was obviously some exercise of will. I didn't get an education by wanting one; I worked for it. These people had become doctors, professional people, importers of Italian accessories. Chuck had gone on to be a stockbroker in Fairbanks, Alaska." And that student he'd met at Oxford, who'd grown up with a blowsy mother and alcoholic stepfather in Arkansas, had just been elected President of the United States. But Chinook left its mark. It was the road not travelled, and he could see it into the distance. "I see several possible outcomes to the life I led then. The worst scenario is prison. I think I was probably not going to let that happen, but who knows? When I read Mikal Gilmore's book, *Shot in The Heart*, about his brother Gary, I was touched by a life that had possibilities not all that different to mine – the way in which these people went from confusion to a criminal rebellion against their luck."

Like half the men in Chinook, Wolff served in Vietnam. He was there during the Tet offensive, a Special Forces lieutenant liaising with the South Vietnamese in the Mekong Delta, when his base came under fire. In the absence of air support, he and his trusted sergeant laid down an artillery barrage so severe that it flattened the town near the camp, killing civilians and Viet Cong alike, firing the big guns so rapidly that by the time darkness fell, the barrels glowed like embers. Although he wrote about Vietnam in the award-winning *In Pharaoh's Army*, he is unwilling to talk about it. In the book, when he tries and fails to explain what it was like to a stranger he'd met in a bar in San Francisco, he offers a partial explanation: "*As soon as you open your mouth ... you have problems, problems of tone, problems of recollection. How can you judge the man now that you've escaped his circumstances, his fears and desires, now that you hardly remember who he was?"* Yet it was in Vietnam, he admits, that he felt the most alive. "We're not talking about joy – that's different, that's watching your children grow – but the simple awareness of the fact of being alive, which I never noticed before to that degree of intensity. When you've been in danger and you get out of it, there's an almost electrical thrum running through you."

At least then, war must have exorcised his love of Hemingway? He looks up, politely professorial, firmly focused on my act of heresy. "In an odd way, I've come to respect him more. He did such a good job writing about war, like in that famous passage at the end of *A Farewell to Arms* where he is talking about the war dead and he says that it's obscene to use abstract words such as glory, honour and courage about them and all you could do was name the places, the regiments and the dates on which they died. That's very true. No-one had said anything like that before. He changed the furniture in the room for everyone.

"It's not a question of exorcising", Wolff explains, "I'm influenced by every writer I've ever loved. I see literature as a great collaboration. I don't see it as individual monuments sticking out of the ground, but a great parade of voices and colours almost in the manner of a medieval cathedral. People came together and made the windows, laid the floor, cut the stone, and all together they made this great thing. That's what's important."

P.S. - *Tobias Wolff's two memoirs,* **This Boy's Life** *and* **In Pharaoh's Army** *are available in paperback, from Bloomsbury and Picador respectively. His short story collection,* **The Night in Question** *and his most recent novel,* **Old School**, *are both published by Bloomsbury in paperback. At the time of writing, an edition of new and selected stories, entitled* **Our Story Begins**, *is due to be published by Bloomsbury in hardback in August 2008.*

Of the other literary works mentioned by Tobias Wolff in this interview, both Mikal Gilmore's **Shot in the Heart** *and Vance Packard's* **The Status Seekers: An Exploration of Class Behaviour in America** *are out of print in the UK at the time of writing. The Chekhov short story is variously translated as "Lady with Dog" "The Lady with the Little Dog", "Lady with Lap Dog", and so on, and is available in numerous paperback editions, as is Hemingway's* **A Farewell to Arms**.

Richard Ford

He's wasn't writing anything at the time, but said that when he does, he'd like to write a short story with a New Jersey setting, "now that I've rid myself of all the Frank Bascombe attachments". We talked a bit about Bascombe, the estate agent protagonist of that great American trilogy that began with 'The Sportswriter' in 1982, because that's what, in July 2007, I'd flown to Dublin to interview Richard Ford about. But then the conversation takes an unplanned turn, towards motivation, resolve – and violence....

VERYONE always asks Richard Ford if he's writing another novel, and right now he's saying no, he mightn't ever write anything again. He might just sit back with a book on the front porch of his Maine lobsterman's house and watch whales, sea eagles and sunsets. Or he might just potter around editing other people's work, or travelling the world giving readings at book festivals and picking up honorary degrees. That's what he's doing when we meet, staying at U2's classily minimalist hotel on the Dublin's increasingly chic Left Bank. A reading tonight at the Abbey Theatre, an honorary degree tomorrow in Cork. The proofs of the collection of American short stories he's editing are already at the printers. *The Lay of the Land*, the last volume of his Frank Bascombe trilogy, was published almost a year ago, and he hasn't written any other fiction since. And, as he says, he might not, ever again.

To understand Ford correctly, you have to realise that this isn't one of those "will-I-won't-I?" statements with which a more fey writer might torment his fans (and, confession time, I'm one: Ford is one of the few writers whose complete works adorn my bookshelves). Ford doesn't do fey. Behind that southern charm and politeness, the sixty-three-year-old American – one of only two to have won both the Pulitzer and the PEN/Faulkner Award for the same novel – has a narrow-eyed intensity of purpose. "Once I put my mind to a thing," he admits, "I have rather a tunnel vision." That's how he started off with *The Sportswriter* twenty-five years ago, with an intensity fuelled by a message from his publisher that, after two well-reviewed but commercially unsuccessful books, unless the next one worked, he was toast. That, and something the Canadian writer Mavis Gallant once said to him: "Richard, if we knew what went on between men and women, we wouldn't need literature." So with his protagonist Frank Bascombe – to my mind, one of the finest fictional creations in modern American fiction – Ford investigated in pointillist detail the emotional core of relationships, those very precise moments at which they might start to gel or to fray. With other writers, Bascombe's introspective exactitude could have veered towards the tiresome – with Ford, this never happens. There are two reasons for this: the long, sweeping cadences and insinuating sinews of Ford's sensuous, thought-filled prose, and the fact he is just as immersed in the minutiae of Bascombe's external life as he is in its inner core.

In other words, when Bascombe moves on from being a sportswriter to being a New Jersey estate agent, Ford takes you completely, four-dimensionally, into that world. Neither New Jersey ("a state that looks like the back of an old radio") nor estate agency have hitherto been the stuff of literary fiction, yet after reading Ford, you wonder why not. Here, just as anywhere else, the American dream forms in house-buyers' minds, as they work out their future moves towards the leafy suburbs or beyond. Bascombe's job is to work out what they want from that future; how he can nudge them towards it, or whether to encourage them to compromise.

We meet in Dublin on the day after a New Hampshire debate in which none of the Republican presidential candidates refused to rule out the idea of nuking Iran. *The Lay of the Land* was written after 9/11, but the one scene of explosive, aimless violence in it wasn't, he insists, any kind of metaphor. "What I was trying to say was that the big changes that took place in America on 9/11 were going on well before then. Violence, an entropic government, a citizenry grown entropic about its responsibilities, a great fear of the other – of immigrants in particular – all were present and building up."

Each of the books in the trilogy, however, is also seeded with violence: with killings that are shown as random and unexplained. I've never heard him talk about that, so I ask if that's his own experience too. "Sure. Violence is an almost daily occurrence in urban America. We've been held up at gunpoint twice in New Orleans. People have attempted to rob me in there too, but I fought them off. But my own experience aside, what I want to describe is what's going on in the background of people's lives, so in the books you'll often catch the echo of a siren going by, see a policeman carrying a firearm, or there'll be something untoward happening. It's just part of life."

After Hurricane Katrina hit New Orleans, Ford spent months there rebuilding houses in the flood-ravaged ninth ward. His wife Kristina had been the city's head of planning until she was forced out by the Republican mayor, about whose efforts to rehouse flood victims Ford is coruscatingly scathing. "We left New Orleans in March fearful for our safety. We were down there for three months this winter and there was so much of an escalation, with police, crooks, murders and violence all around, that we began to think, 'We have to get out of here before something happens to us.' We were thinking, the odds would catch up with us, how stupid we would feel ... all my friends were saying, 'Get out of there,' because they knew I was working in dangerous places."

He tells me about the last time he was mugged. A beggar had asked him for money, and attacked him as he reached for his wallet. They fell together to the ground, with Ford, by chance, landing on top. "I just started pounding him," he says, slamming a first into his open palm. "It was just instinctive." The sound of his fist lingers in the comfortable quiet of the hotel room. He'd done the same thing when he told me the story of the moment he realised that Kristina

— a willowy, elegant woman who joins us a few minutes later — was the love of his life. He's told it before, but it's so impossibly romantic I can't help asking him to tell it to me again.

They met in Michigan when he was nineteen and she was seventeen, and vowed to get married the year she graduated. They didn't. Ford went off to teach, Kristina to a job in New York, where she soon acquired a new boyfriend. Missing her "like crazy", he got on a plane to New York and caught a taxi to her apartment, where he arrived, without warning, at ten o'clock at night. "I didn't know if her boyfriend was going to be there when I turned up." I clench my fists and hold them up in front of my face. "Don't think that wouldn't have happened," he laughs. That was in January. They married in March. They've been together "for forty-four years, longer than you've been alive". Such a charmer, being deliberately wrong by a decade.

But the suddenness of that slapped fist somehow lingers in the conversation. He's already told me about the fights he used to get into, growing up in Mississippi: "In the schoolyards, in the weekends, in front of the bowling alley, rites of passage stuff." In the cuttings, I've read the other story people repeat about Ford: how he once shot a hole through a copy of a book by novelist Alice Hoffman, who'd given *The Sportswriter* a damning review, and had posted it off to her publisher. He's also already told me how he joined the marines in 1964, straight after taking his postgraduate English degree. An odd choice, I thought at the time, given that Vietnam had just started, but he doesn't see anything special about it. He's already talked about his love of boxing, and how he used to hero-worship fighters such as Thomas Hearns and others from the Kronk gym in Detroit; about the times he met Muhammad Ali. Oddly, although it's his favourite sport, he didn't write much about boxing in his sportswriting days.

He didn't need to. That same intensity is written all over his early fiction; always has been, right from the day he met Raymond

Carver, who became his closest friend, at a writers' conference in Texas in 1977. The sparseness of the language of his short stories – a style that for a while was known as "dirty realism" – drips with it. You don't get that from the novels, you might think. But look again. Those ornate descriptions, somehow at once precise and sweeping. They sound right because Ford reads them out aloud as he writes – he's a superb reader of his work – reading the whole book out loud to Kristina as he nears the final revise. He works on the writing, like a boxer in the gym: focused, intent. It doesn't come easy, either the inspiration or the writing. He is, he reveals, dyslexic. How many other dyslexic writers do you know? I ask. "There are loads," he says. "Loads." But no, he can't name any offhand.

If reading or writing is a daily small fight, though, it squares off with my overall picture of Richard Ford: intense, battling, driven – yet also charming, courteous, and writing with great emotional precision. Add all that to the high cheekbones and pale blue eyes, and can get you an inkling of his appeal. He hadn't meant to talk so much about fighting, he says. I nod and mention that it's something I know little about, having never thrown a punch in anger since I was seven. "I'm not sure if that's a good thing or a bad thing," he grins. And now that he mentions it, neither am I.

P.S. - *Richard Ford's six novels,* **The Ultimate Good Luck** *(1981),* **The Sportswriter** *(1986),* **A Piece of My Heart** *(1987),* **Wildlife** *(1990),* **Independence Day** *(1995) and* **The Lay of the Land** *(2006), his two short story collections* **Rock Springs** *(1987) and* **A Multitude of Sins** *(2002), and the collection of three novellas* **Women with Men** *(1997), are all available from Bloomsbury in paperback.*

At the time of writing, **The New Granta Book of the American Short Story***, edited by Richard Ford, is available only in hardback. Richard Ford's* **Writers' Workshop in a Book** *is published by Chronicle Books.*

Looking for Rebus

Working out who committed the murder and why is, he says, the least interesting aspect of the crime novel; far more important is its ability to hold up a mirror to society. Few writers have done this more skilfully - or more profitably - than the creator of the (now retired) DI John Rebus. Yet when you follow Ian Rankin's path to becoming Britain's bestselling crimewriter, the clues are hardly straightforward at all ...

JANUARY, 2008. One of those rare Saturdays on which I've wrenched my fifteen-year-old son away from his Playstation. I promise him a mystery tour, and we head into the centre of Edinburgh. I'm expecting a degree of resistance when I lead him into the National Library of Scotland, but I've already sold him on the horrors within. There will be a book with its cover made out of a hanged man's skin, I tell him, along with the death mask of a murderer, with a visible rope-mark on the neck. "Crime Scene Edinburgh", the exhibition is called. It will, I assure him, be exactly like *CSI Miami*, only a bit more local.

What I don't add, because he hasn't yet read any of Ian Rankin's books, is that the exhibition – celebrating twenty years since the publication of *Noughts and Crosses* – could just as easily be called "Looking for Rebus". And I don't mention that, six years before, when I first interviewed Rankin, that's just what I'd been doing too. To get inside a mind as complex and imagined as Rankin's, you need a few clues. To make it easier, imagine the process as a picture puzzle. A rebus, in other words.

In 2001, when I met Rankin for the first time, to talk about his novel *The Falls*, the rebus I envisaged was made up of three very different, seemingly unconnected images, with a possible red herring among them. A comic made by an eight-year-old child. A central heating engineer in an Edinburgh bar on Friday nights. A copy of *The Scotsman* dated 19 September 1983. Let's begin with the last, because that's where Rankin's first short story – about a factory closure in Fife – appeared after he was named as one of the winners of a competition. He won a Sinclair Spectrum computer (memory: 48K) for third prize. But because a rebus is usually symbolic, here the newspaper stands for all the media interest in him.

Imagine fame as a Catherine wheel. Light the fuse with your first book and it starts spinning round you, a shower of sparks quickly forming into a ring of light, each successful book, each interview and headline making the circle that little bit brighter. By the time I meet Rankin in 2001, his own circle of fame was glowing bright. He was already a one-man multi-national, his diary blocked off for months ahead, his mobile phone constantly ringing with requests. A spot of punditry perhaps for *Newsnight Late Review?* A radio show about Brits who have lived abroad? Small flurries of calls from harassed newsdesks: "It's about the latest rise in crime figures, Mr Rankin. Would you care to comment?" His publisher wanting him at their table for the British Book Awards, or scheduling book tours to the antipodes. "Er, Ian, we were thinking about a *South Bank Show* profile..." Her Majesty requesting the pleasure of his company for a reception at Buckingham Palace. Committees, causes, charities: for a man with so many pressures on his time, he gives swathes of it to other people.

That Catherine wheel spun slowly at first. In 1986, when he signed the deal for *Noughts and Crosses* with Orion, they were just starting out too, with offices in Anthony Cheetham's living-room. Rankin has stayed with them ever since, and the seventeen carefully rebranded covers on display in the National Library exhibition are proof of his loyalty. My son walks straight past them, bored by marketing, towards the DIY forensic desk on the other side of the room. I worry that he is growing listless, so I tell him about my first interview with Ian Rankin, all those years ago, how he'd popped into a bank as we walked across Edinburgh city centre to a restaurant. He wouldn't be long, he said, he just had to sign a few papers.

Just a couple of minutes should do it. I waited outside. Over lunch, he told me what he'd been doing. To keep him from the clutches of rivals Transworld, Orion had offered him a £1.3 million two-book deal – then a record for any Scottish author – and he had decided to form his own company, John Rebus Ltd. As he was its chief executive and sole employee, he had to sign a few forms at the bank. The manager asked him what kind of salary he wanted to pay himself. He'd never thought much about it, so he quickly worked out his main expenses. "Er ... how about £15,000?" The bank manager laughed. In hindsight, with Rankin accountable for one-tenth of all crime fiction sales in the UK, Orion's deal sounds, if anything, a little on the conservative side.

Back in the early 1990s, Rankin, then living in the Dordogne, had to write two books a year to earn even a meagre income. By the time of his big breakthrough with his Macallan Gold Dagger award-winning *Black and Blue* in 1997, he already had eight Rebus novels in the bag. Suddenly, he was in the kind of position every author dreams of: not only were the new novels automatic best-sellers, so, belatedly, were the old ones. The Catherine wheel of fame started spinning ever faster. Televised versions of Rebus filled the two-hour prime-time Sunday night slot previously occupied by Inspector Morse. While Morse was killed off by his creator Colin Dexter in 2000, the equally irascible and hard-drinking Rebus survived until he was officially pensioned off in 2007's *Exit Music*.

Meanwhile, the fan base was building. Go into Rebus's – and Rankin's – favourite howff, the Oxford Bar, and you are just as likely to find Rankin's international brigade of readers as the man himself. This is the hard core of fandom, the kind of people who read Rebus novels with an Edinburgh A-Z close at hand, and come to the city in search of landmarks. ("Look, that's Oxford Terrace - that's where Rebus's girlfriend lived in *Set in Darkness*. " "Those converted flats by the Water of Leith? Remember dodgy Detective Derek Linford? Just the right place for a yuppie cop like him." "Heriot Row? Well he doesn't spell it out, but that brothel in *Strip Jack* ... it could really be there, behind that douce late Georgian facade of Craigleith sandstone ...") Those are the fans, that is the media whorl. Yet somewhere in the middle was a writer wondering whether he can keep up, a writer learning to live with the biggest irony of media celebrity: that the more successful you become, the less time you have for writing the books that made you successful in the first place.

The second clue in my rebus had the kind of odds against it that would make any bookie shudder. It's to do with the name of Rankin's fictional detective, which he chose back in 1986, when his first novel, *The Flood*, was published. Too many people spotted the obviously autobiographical elements in its story of a teenager growing up in a small Fife mining village, dreaming of escape to the metropolis, so Rankin set about creating a character with whom he definitely could not be confused: not just a policeman, but a policeman who was married, with a car and a mortgage. Someone a million miles away from a precociously bright working-class student researching a PhD on Muriel Spark at Edinburgh University; a novice writer with a strong interest in semiotics and deconstruction. And because his first crime novel, *Noughts and Crosses* relied on picture puzzle clues, when he came upon the dictionary definition of the word "rebus" it seemed a perfect name for his fictional detective. No-one would be called that, surely?

A decade passed and Rankin returned to Edinburgh from his six-year working exile in France. Just take a moment to ponder the sheer unlikelihood of what followed. According to the telephone directories, there are only two people in the whole of Scotland called Rebus, and they are father and son. Joe Rebus just happens to live on Rankin Avenue, Edinburgh. When they were introduced, Rankin was convinced it was a wind-up. But they became friends, meeting up after work on Friday in a southside pub as part of a group that also includes an horologist, a bookseller, an office worker, a retired policeman, a refrigeration engineer and an ITV cameraman. Joe Rebus – the "e" is short as in "bell" – is a central heating engineer. He's the same age as his fictional namesake, but otherwise has nothing in common with him. In this particular rebus, Joe Rebus might seem a red herring. But if you stood at the bar, listening to the relaxed conversation between the men about the day's events, the weekend's sport and the usual inspired nonsenses of Friday night banter, you'd be hard pressed to work out just which of them is the successful writer. Which is exactly as it should be, but seldom is.

Before Rankin dreamed up Rebus, modern Scottish crime fiction barely existed. William McIlvanney had written his three *Laidlaw* novels, Muriel Spark had turned the genre on its head with her elegant novella *The Driver's Seat*, but its possibilities remained barely explored. Rebus changed that. His first outing, in *Noughts and Crosses* wasn't written as a crime novel: Rankin was, he has said, aiming more at "Stevenson at his darkest", and at an Edinburgh version of *Laidlaw*. It was only when it had been reviewed as crime fiction, and he had been asked to join the Crime Writers' Association, that Rankin realised he had inadvertently become a genre writer. By *Black and Blue*, however, Rebus had emerged as a more fully formed character. Unlike the little old lady amateur sleuths of the classical English tradition, who were emotionally unchanged by the tragedies their job uncovered, here was a thrawn detective who was affected by what he saw, yet who almost needed to concentrate on the minutiae of other people's lives to keep him from looking at the emptiness within his own.

What better pair of eyes was there to see Scotland through? Rebus could peer into that part of Edinburgh that the tourist never sees; walk the mean streets of the housing schemes where HIV rates were the worst in Europe yet also have access to the highest figures in the land. He could find himself in a urine-stained alleyway in Leith one minute, a merchant banker's boardroom in Charlotte Square the next. It is all, Rankin insists, just a matter of empathy.

If he hadn't been the first person in his family to go to university, his own life could have run a similar course to Rebus's. Rosyth dockyard, the police, the army: those were the main career options for his schoolmates growing up across the Forth in Cardenden – "Car-dead-end", they called it – in the years after the mines shut down. Rebus joined the army, then the police. In an alternative past, perhaps Rankin would have done too. And then what? Perhaps, like Rebus, he would resent those fast-tracked graduates who shot so far ahead of him; those closed (but computer-literate) minds which did not see how readily good can leech into evil, people who were sheltered – as he is not – from the knowledge that, fundamentally, there's not too much difference between them and the villains they track down. For Rankin, Rebus serves other purposes. All the guilt, embarrassment, frustration and anger at the things that go wrong in his own life can be offloaded onto his fictional alter ego. He can stick Rebus's daughter in a wheelchair, make him investigate war crimes, let him shoulder the burden of discovering a paedophile ring, pile up whole battalions of troubles on him. Rankin uses Rebus, he admits, exactly as Rebus uses his own job: as a distraction from his own fears and worries.

But here's a mystery about Rebus. Everyone thinks they know what he looks like, but everyone is wrong. Rankin can tell us exactly what is going on in his brain, but cannot – and never has – put a face to him. Nor does he want to. Why not? I wonder if that's the biggest clue so far.

Reviewing *Exit Music* in *The Scotsman*, Allan Massie pointed out that not only had Rankin "produced the most sustained body of fiction devoted to modern Edinburgh, but has made it once again a city of the mind as Dickens made London and Chandler Los Angeles. He has changed the way people imagine the city." Rankin's public identification with the city is equally deep. It's in Edinburgh, rather than in Buckingham Palace, that he chose to be invested with the OBE; its charities, competitions and literary life that he routinely supports. Edinburgh made him and he doesn't forget his debts. It was there, at university, that he read Chandler and Ellroy, and it was to Edinburgh that his mind constantly returned when he was in the Dordogne writing those early Rebus novels, learning to edge his books with a frisson of reality that somehow never slides off into parochialism.

The last Rebus rebus, the final Rankin clue, isn't from Edinburgh at all. It's a comic that an eight-year-old boy drew in Cardenden. He'd take a piece of paper, fold and cut it to make an eight-page booklet, fill it with stories with bubbles for words above the characters' heads and make a "free" badge to stick on the front. He'd show it to his mother. She'd look at it bemusedly and hand it back. He wasn't ever, he admits, particularly good at drawing. Three years later, the boy discovered music. Listening to it wasn't enough: he had to invent a whole band. His father brought back a ledger from the shop where he worked in Lochgelly and he wrote up the story of a group called the Amoebas, starring himself as Ian Kaput, the lead singer. In that ledger, he drew pictures of the band, with details of all their members. He wrote out all their lyrics, where they went on tour, and scripted their *Parkinson* appearance. Every week he prepared a top ten singles and albums chart for which he had to invent nine other bands, all their band members, and all their album covers. He didn't tell his mother about writing the lyrics. He didn't tell anyone. But when he was fifteen, there was a poetry competition at school and he entered. The first his parents and two sisters knew about it was when they read the *Dundee Courier* headline "Local Boy Wins Poetry Competition". It was only second prize actually, but it was worth £5.

"What I was doing," Ian Rankin told me, on that dreich spring day in Edinburgh when he had just become a one-man company, "is creating a world where I can play God, over which I had complete control. There's a great sense of power and self-satisfaction in creating a world where you can make anything happen." He was talking about that Cardenden schoolboy, but he could just as easily have been talking about moving DI John Rebus around the dark, secret heart of Edinburgh, setting demons on him that a pint at the Oxford Bar and a half bottle of Bell's from the off-licence never quite remove; loading him with guilt he can only push away by following a line of cold reason wherever it leads away from the scene of a crime.

So although the final clue yields the most truth, it is not a complete answer to the Rebus rebus. Rankin's wife Miranda and two sons would have other, better ones. Seven men having a pint last night at a southside bar in Edinburgh might have come closer. So might the tourists who come to the Oxford Bar and other real stop-offs in Rankin's far more dramatic and dangerous fictional city. As for me, I have just one thought to add. It's this: that if you are playing God, the last thing you want to show is the artifice of your creation, the strings that move the puppets. If Rankin could imagine what Rebus looked like, Rebus's Edinburgh would be less real, less vivid, less involving. Out of focus himself, the detective retains a mystery that puts the mystery of his case in the sharpest focus of all.

Kate Atkinson

She rarely gives newspaper interviews, so I was delighted when Kate Atkinson agreed to talk to me about her latest novel, the exquisitely funny and tightly plotted 'One Good Turn: A Jolly Murder Mystery'. It's set in the city where we both live, and opens with a road rage incident in a street I walk to work on every day. We met in July 2006, as Edinburgh was gearing up for the Festival which also forms the backdrop to her novel.

SK ALI SMITH what she thinks of Kate Atkinson's writing and the words pour out in a torrent of rapture. "No-one else remotely like her: Jane Austen crossed with a 21st-century Laurence Sterne; sheer unadulterated brilliance; people don't even begin to realise just how good she is". OK, you might think: Smith is a generous critic. She's also one of Atkinson's friends, singled out for particular thanks in her last novel, *Case Histories*, so perhaps she's biased. And then you read *One Good Turn*, and you realise Smith got it right. Nor is she alone in rating Atkinson so highly: some months ago Stephen King wrote that *Case Histories* was "not just the best novel I read this year, but the best mystery of the decade".

The woman whose books inspire such swooning praise is a reluctant interviewee. It's not that she's withdrawn: on the contrary, she's great company. She just doesn't see the point of interviews, or at least not the ones she's had in the past, when she's been asked such questions as whether her mother has Alzheimer's, whether she's ever given a child away for adoption, what her own children think about her writing, or how often she has sex. "It's astonishing, this need that people have for you to be something more than just the anonymous author of a book," she says. "Yet what is it about an author that really makes them interesting? The text, nothing more. I hate it when I hear writers talking about what they think. Why should that matter any more than what anyone else thinks?"

So, to the text then. Atkinson's bursts with wit, sharp intelligence, and percipience. Here is an author who can plot a triptych of murders to perfection, not only within the tightest of time frames but also whilst dividing the narrative between four voices: Gloria, middle-aged wife of a dodgy millionaire builder; Louise, an Edinburgh police inspector and mother of a wayward adolescent; former private eye Jackson Brodie, the main protagonist in *Case Histories*, now retired and rich; and the spectacularly ineffectual crime novelist Martin Canning. Unlike *Case Histories*, which although still lit up with Atkinson's pinpoint wit, was far more darkly tragic, *One Good Turn* is every bit as jolly as its subtitle proclaims. It is the kind of book whose margins you can't help littering with delighted squiggles or exclamation marks, so perfectly are even its most grotesque characters drawn; so accurate even its minor details. Even for those who've never lived through Edinburgh in August (which, come to think of it, has hitherto been very badly served by fiction), it's great fun.

It's playfully complex too. When she shows us the mild-mannered Merchiston crime writer Martin Canning, for example, she also introduces the main voice in his head: that of Nina Riley, the 1940s good-gal heroine of his inoffensive fiction. Atkinson has great fun with pastiche here, but she also gives Martin a halfway-plausible backstory, and trails a real-life tragedy caused by his brief fling with a seller of matryoshka dolls. That's just one character and just one voice, but three very different types of writing. So this is a rich, layered, text, sparkling with originality, ornate plotting and literary ventriloquism. Martin might dream of writing something intricate and experimental himself, but he knows he never will: he's just about given up on life and writes fiction that reflects his resignation. Then, right at the end, as she does with all her main characters, Atkinson swipes once more at the predictable with a final, satisfying stir of the plot.

It seems effortless, and in a sense it was. "I've learnt to write within the internal monologue, within character, and once you've got that character's voice, you slip into it easily," she says. The only problem was that after finishing *Case Histories*, ("the easiest book I've ever written"), she was ready to plough straight into another novel featuring her ex-army, ex-police, ex-private eye Jackson Brodie, but she feared it would look too much like a sequel. Publishers were already talking about "another Jackson Brodie mystery", which was the last thing she wanted. Instead, she embarked on an abortive novel featuring both Martin and Gloria ("the one character I've written so far who's most like me") that grew to four hundred pages and took a year out of her life before she decided to put it out of its misery.

When she started *One Good Turn* she knew immediately what its structure, and what its feel, would be. It would begin with all the characters in a scene together – either in, or witnessing, a road rage incident in Edinburgh's Cowgate. After that they'd all scatter and come together in the finale. But this time she already had the characters of Martin and Gloria from the abortive novel. Jackson Brodie had walked across from *Case Histories*, so Louise the Edinburgh detective was the only missing link, "a bit of a challenge at first but easy once I'd got the hang of her".

Writing with four such distinct voices not only freed her style, it took care of the structure, too. Already she'd explored all the blind alleys she needed to with the Martin and Gloria characters, so this time she knew roughly what direction she was going in as she switched from character to character. This is the point at which graft and craft mix. Because all the plot takes place over three days in the one city, the characters cross each others' paths, invisible to each other, and the same scenes are frequently shown from different characters' viewpoints. But then there's even more going on, because with Atkinson, character, observation and plot all grow entwined. Before she starts a novel, she says, she never knows how the story is going to resolve itself: "Why bother - that would just be too boring." In any case, she likes there to be an element of mystery-solving in anything she writes, and that goes for the writing process itself.

Atkinson doesn't go in for plot diagrams either. It's all in her head, not just when she's physically writing but all the time she's working on a book. The best way to understand how she wrote *One Good Turn* is probably to imagine four bars on a computer graph, each one representing one of the main characters, each edging up one at a time, keeping pace with each other. "You're constantly edging the narrative forward in one voice, always on the front edge because you don't know what's going to happen, and you have an instinctive knowledge about how far you want each of them to go. You want a feeling of completeness with each section, a rhythm and structure and — most importantly — shape to it, and only then can you move the story on again."

But as Atkinson gives examples of how scenes open up and allow new ones to form, I start to have doubts — not about writing, where I am effectively being treated to a detailed masterclass in the complexity of mixing character and plot — but about her insistence that the text is absolutely everything. Of course, it's presumptuous to imagine that an hour's chat with anyone can reveal all their innermost secrets. It's equally absurd — insulting even — to imagine that writing springs fully formed out of experience, as a host of interviewers have wrongly presumed was the case with Atkinson, ever since her remarkable *Behind the Scenes at the Museum* won the Whitbread Book of the Year in 1995. But surely the text stems from what one person has put together from life? Atkinson tells me that her next book will take Jackson to Paris: "Yes, I may have to live there for a while — it's a tough life".

Still further down the track, she is contemplating a novel in which Jackson Brodie returns to his Yorkshire roots to try to find out who murdered his sister. And as she says that, Atkinson is quite open about the fact that she will also be addressing part of her own family's history too. The only reason she hasn't yet done it, she tells me, is not because there are any great secrets to deal with but simply because she hasn't yet fully worked out what her attitude to it is. "But I do want to bring some of that to bear on Jackson, to give him part of my history," she says. "Because he must have part of me to succeed as a character. They all must." So the best text isn't just text, it's life too. And with *One Good Turn*, it's life as a tightly wound, absolutely irresistible comedy.

P.S. - One Good Turn, Case Histories, Behind the Scenes at the Museum, Human Croquet, Emotionally Weird and *Atkinson's collection of short stories, **Not the End of the World**, are all published in paperback by Black Swan.*

One Good Turn *was shortlisted for the British Book Awards Crime Thriller of the Year..*

Ali Smith

Ali Smith is a friend. She's warm-hearted, thoughtful, intelligent, good fun to be with. She's also impossibly modest: impressively so, given the number of literary prizes she's either won or been shortlisted for, at events where we invariably meet. Of all the pieces I've written about her, this — from 2001, when I interviewed her in Cambridge about her latest collection of short stories — is the one that best conveys the essential qualities of her writing: its absence of ego, as well as its intellectual playfulness.

I N THE opening of one of the short stories in *The Whole Story and Other Stories*, Ali Smith's new collection, a character asks, "What do you need to know about me for this story? How old I am? How much I earn a year? What kind of car I drive?" The answers, in her own case, are 39, not as much as you'd think, and a second-hand Rover. What else do you need to know about Ali Smith? She was born in Inverness, went to university in Aberdeen, lives in Cambridge. She's an academic-turned-writer who has published two previous collections of short stories and two novels, each shortlisted for at least one major prize. Her break-through novel, *Hotel World*, sold 100,000 copies in Britain. It was shortlisted in 2002 for the Man Booker and the Orange prizes, won both the Scottish Arts Council Book of the Year Award and the Encore Award. Her third novel, *The Accidental*, achieved similar sales, and won the 2005 Whitbread Novel Award. More? She's a lesbian and has been with her partner, Sarah, for two decades. They live in a terraced house next to the one in which cricket legend Jack Hobbes was born: she has books everywhere, an enormous cat, and there's a sycamore tree above her study window. Why did she become a writer? She had chronic fatigue syndrome twelve years ago, so she quit lecturing at Strathclyde University in 1992 and was immobilised for months. One hot June day, sitting on a bench in

Edinburgh's Royal Botanic Gardens, she wrote a short story – and it poured out of her so fast that her hand still hurt from writing it three days later. She entered it for Scotland's biggest short story competition. When it won, she found the confidence to try making a living as a full-time writer.

Was there any hint of any of this in her childhood? Ah, now, wait... She's sitting in my hotel room in Cambridge, talking into a tape machine on the table between us, remembering growing up in Inverness. "My mother was a tree surgeon," she explains. "She loved trees so much that she lived in one most of the time. And the rest of my creative family, we'd be sitting underneath the tree, and she'd cut off the twigs from the top branches and send them down to let us know when it was time for us to have tea. Only the tips she didn't want to grow, obviously. One day there was a procession of people from the local church passing by the tree, and the man in black said, 'You shouldn't be up that tree, lassie! You should get down immediately!' My mother refused. She was adamant. And I'm sure that's marked my life ever since and made me an imaginative writer." Really? No, not really. Not at all, in fact. But Smith had done an interview the previous day and, for two hours, she'd been asked about being a lesbian, and why and how about chronic fatigue syndrome, and how and why about coming from a small town in Scotland. And, yes, there was one, just the one, question about her new book. And sometimes – in fact, often – she gets depressed about what that says about our culture, that we don't look at the writing but only at the writer, that we never get beyond the surface of things. So the next time someone asks, she may well start inventing an entire past life. A tree surgeon mother, for example.

Why? Because the life's got nothing to do with the work. Or rather, there may be one or two common threads – and these are what interviewers always pick up on. In *Hotel World*, for example, one of the characters has ME and Smith's had chronic fatigue syndrome; another worked as a style journalist and Smith herself had briefly helped out at her brother's advertising agency; another worked as a receptionist, as she'd done herself for a summer job; then the main character and Smith's partner both have the same first name, and there's a potential gay love affair in it and Smith herself is gay and ..."And look at what that does to the book," she says. "It breaks its bones. It takes it apart, splays it out and says there is a reason for everything in this art. There's a closedness about it that makes me angry. Because it looks as though there's an equation: this person is gay, therefore they write in a certain way, this person is a man, therefore he must write in a certain way. To me, that kind of thinking is like a trap in the forest that catches the leg of an animal. The leg might be left there in the trap, you might have caught it, but you can't see the whole animal running. There's an Emily Dickinson poem, 'Split the lark'. 'Split the lark,' it says, 'cut down into the middle of it, see what's inside.' Well, that's not the essence of the lark, of its soaring, unsingable strangeness. And that's why the biographical trail is always a false one. It may seem interesting, but it doesn't lead anywhere."

True, there are some writers from whom that line of argument shouldn't be accepted. If Hemingway goes to Spain and writes about what he saw and how it changed him, the life obviously informs the work. But Smith doesn't operate like that: when she sits down to write, she says, her own ego only gets in the way. "I've got to forget about it, wait for it to recede, wait until I can let the stories go where they want to go." And no, she doesn't even want to think about how she actually does that, in case it stops her from doing it again. Yet when that Smith ego fades away, just look at what's left behind. In *Hotel World*, there are scenes of homelessness, illness, bereavement and bleak consumerism; and scenes from the edge of life itself. The opening, which is narrated by a ghost already starting to lose its grip on language and memory, is one of the most beautiful and startling novelistic beginnings I've read in years.

And now here she is again, with a collection of short stories that is even bolder, even riskier, and still all the journalists want to know about is this lesbian, Scottish, used-to-be-ill person who wrote them. She's bored with that. Bored with the fringes of celebrity culture, with the necessary circus of prizes, even the delightful surrealism of the Booker night, which she describes as "rather like being on a 1950s cruise ship with luxurious food, alcohol that doesn't stop and old-world manners: you expect to see a young Gore Vidal turn the corner or the young Muriel Spark surrounded by gentlemanly cads, all smoking long blue-smoke cigarettes". Bored with the way in which, as she writes in her new collection, "The face and the voice and the name, the body of the writer, are sold as part of the £9.99 package. Tiny peeled slivers of him and her inserted for years between the pages like erratum slips or bookmarks." If that sounds overly precious, it's not. Smith is among the most intellectually generous of writers, an evangelist for other authors she admires. After our interview, I go along to a reading she gives with Jackie Kay at the Cambridge Book Festival. At the end of the event, she reads a story from her new collection. But then, rather than plug her own work, she tells the audience that the one book they really ought to buy is Kay's latest.

Both are collections of short stories, an art form to which Smith is passionately committed but which she fears is desperately under threat. Publishers don't like them, only occasionally bother to market them, and constantly put pressure on writers to produce novels instead. Even poetry gets more support: whilst major prizes such as the Whitbread recognise poetry, they don't even have a category for short stories. Writing them in Britain today, she says, can be a short cut to oblivion. And not just in the "Numpty Noughties" – she notes that when Katherine Mansfield published her first collection, Virginia Woolf wrote in her diary, "She's done for now!" Yet, if you look at what Smith can do with the short story, you see what we may be missing. Of the twelve in *The Whole Story*, there's hardly one that doesn't risk something new, that doesn't take a leap, that doesn't ooze confidence. Which is odd, because Smith is never confident about anything she writes. On finishing *Hotel World*, she thought it too dark and would have chucked it in the bin, had Sarah not disagreed.

In *The Whole Story*, Smith's stories crack and break open, taking you in a completely different direction to where you may have imagined they were heading. In some, the course of a relationship is charted in two first-person narratives, completing conversations, giving what might appear to be the whole story. In others, those conversations are broken into, like mobile phone calls interrupted by tunnels or multi-channel grazing, TV zapper in hand. "That's important," says Smith, "because we live on a surface that we think is controllable. We think we can talk to anybody at any time, or learn things at random from TV, and be in control. And the war in Iraq, for example, has shown us how that's a complete joke, that we're all living on this crazy surface pretending that nothing very much is happening. Whereas, really, everything is happening and we can't even see it, and we're so spun that we can't get off the surface."

Getting off the surface is something Smith's stories do effortlessly. Their original triggers of inspiration are often slight: an apple tree infested with ants, sycamore seeds drumming down on her study window, an odd-looking man dressed in white in King's Cross station, a couple of chance remarks, a newspaper article about the Highlands being the best place to live in Britain. But look what happens then. The man dressed in white in King's Cross, for example, becomes Death; the Grim Reaper transformed into someone who looks like a BBC arts executive, and Death is indeed on the line, further up, in a brilliant story that leaves the cold rails of realism and a superficially-controlled life far behind. And the tree, well, that may be just an obsession, something a lover has fallen in love with, will sacrifice anything for, something the partner can't possibly understand, or it may be just a beautiful image of love. Or both.

To Smith, it doesn't matter. Images don't have to be tied down. Nor, in at least three of the stories about relationships, does the protagonist's gender. To what extent is that because she wants to avoid being pigeonholed as a Scottish lesbian writer? "You mean the myth of Smith," she says and laughs. "You know," she continues, "although those things – Scottish lesbian or whatever – might sound more exotic, what I am really is just a booky geek." I'm thinking back to what she told me about the collection, about how the main story is called "Paradise" because she'd just been reading and comparing translations of Dante's *Inferno* – just for fun, you understand. And how "The Universal Story", which opens the book, had its origins in a thought that drifted into her mind while she was looking at Sarah's collection of different editions of *The Great Gatsby* – "She's a booky geek too, that's why we love each other". About the girl growing up in Inverness, youngest of five children, who was reading *Gulliver's Travels* and writing her own poetry book at the age of eight. Her mother, a switchboard operator and a bus conductress before she fell ill with angina, would have noticed this booky geekishness early on, but her parents didn't go out of their way to encourage it. "Are you joking?" says Smith. "They thought I was weird." But when you talk with her, the geek is barely evident, drowned out by the fervour with which she discusses other writers, the enthusiasm that bubbles up into her conversation whenever you mention an author whose work she loves. Books figure in each of the twelve stories in the collection. In a few of them, love is there, too. "Books and love," she says. "That'd make a great title for the autobiography - Books, Love and A Few Lies." And she throws back her head and laughs.

So what else do you need to know about Ali Smith? That she likes Turkish food and whisky, though not together? That she cried watching the opening of the Scottish Parliament, "though I'd just as easily cry at the Corries singing 'The Road to Dundee'"? That she still speaks with a soft Inverness accent, even though a story in the new collection is the first time she has written in it since she was at school? What else? You mean, what's she like? Funny, kind, friendly, inventive, passionate, original, radical. The kind of person no-one has a bad word for. Unless you think a booky geek is a bad thing to be. And even then, it's not the whole story.

P.S. - *Ali Smith's most recent book is* **Girl Meets Boy**, *a contemporary re-working of the myth of Iphis, published by Canongate.* **Hotel World, The Accidental, The Whole Story and Other Stories** *are all available in paperback from Penguin. Smith's first novel* **Like**, *and first collection of short stories,* **Free Love and Other Stories**, *are available in paperback from Virago. Ali Smith has also written a play,* **The Seer**, *which is published by Faber.*

Jackie Kay

Of all the authors I know, Jackie Kay is the one whose autobiography I most want to read. I want to learn more about that childhood with her wonderful adoptive parents in Glasgow's communist subculture, and find out just when it was that she became what she is today — one of the most joyously life-enhancing writers around. Our paths cross at various literary events, and I am always glad when they do. But this, in 2001, was the first time.

ACKIE KAY is telling me stories from her life. Like how, when she was eleven, she wrote a novel about a black girl who passed for white and who travelled across America having adventures. "I called it One Person, Two Names," she says, smiling knowingly back across the table at me. She knows what to expect from journalists interviewing her about her latest book: how we'll arrive in Manchester, with an hour or two to sum up her whole life, and how we invariably write about writers in an odd way, forcing obtuse links between the person and the work, blind to imagination. She knows we are prurient ferrets, especially when confronted with black lesbian mothers like her; that the personal and the intimate and the out-of-the-ordinary are red meat to us. 'One Person, Two Names.' Yes, she's probably thinking, that's him off sewing my life together. *'Even at the age of eleven, Jackie Kay was already exploring questions of identity; even in a primary school exercise book she was wondering what she would have been like if she hadn't been adopted by a white couple. Thirty years later, she is still wondering...'* Actually, I'm not thinking that at all. But since her stunning debut novel, *Trumpet*, had featured an intrusive hack journalist trying to ferret out a sensationalist angle on what is really a haunting story of love and loss, I might as well get the clichés out of the way now.

What I'm really thinking is that this stylish, attractive, vivacious, slightly hung-over woman sitting across from me in a Manchester restaurant writes about what Baudelaire called "the wings of madness" better than anyone else I've read. Why? I ask. It turns out there is no reason – at least none of those blatantly obvious reasons we ferrets prefer. Neither she nor anyone close to her has slipped off the tightrope of sanity as comprehensively and frighteningly as the protagonist of "The Woman With Knife and Fork Disorder" in her debut short-story collection *Why Don't You Stop Talking*. No-one she knows has anything remotely like the terrible condition of the woman in the title story, who says exactly what she thinks, even to complete strangers, and realises only too late that what's inside her head just doesn't square with what is outside. If there is a link between Kay and these women, she says, it lies in the way we live now. "People are more compulsive and neurotic than they were just twenty years ago. In the absence of any real sense of community, we have all these media-driven panics where everyone gets obsessed by something like BSE, anthrax, MMR jabs, or when our feelings get out of control so quickly, as they did over Diana's death. Their obsessions might be different, but these characters just reflect their times."

In all the stories, the writing is spare, deceptively simple, dynamic. Kay says short stories suit her, and on this evidence she is right. Her portraits of women on the verge of insanity or love are like short balloon voyages soaring straight up into the clouds of bliss or despair: any longer and they might crash back to earth, or go too far and expire in thin air. Instead, the voyage ends at the precise point that allows it to carry on in the reader's mind. Weeks after reading the collection, they are still haunting mine. Although most of the fourteen stories have protagonists who are either lesbian or black, their links with Kay's own life aren't always distinct. We're back, it seems, with the ferret's natural enemies, imagination and understanding. In Kay's case, the only way to uncover the link between the writer and the work is to go right back into her past. All the way back.

Kay made that journey – and established her reputation – with the partly autobiographical *The Adoption Papers*, her 1991 debut collection of poetry. It tells the story of a black girl's adoption by a white Scottish couple from three different points of view: the mother, the birth-mother and the daughter. Tender and flooded with empathy, it is charged with depth yet wonderfully accessible, and was a universally popular winner of both the Saltire and Forward Prizes.

Kay's partner, the poet Carol Ann Duffy[*], has a brilliant image about parenthood. It is, she says, as if you suddenly discover another room in your house, a room you had never seen before or suspected existed, and when you open its door, you enter to find it bathed in light. In *The Adoption Papers*, Kay imagines how her parents prepared for that extra room of light. How, once they'd said that they didn't mind which colour their baby was, the waiting list seemed to vanish. How, although they were Communists, they took down all signs of party membership before the woman from the adoption agency came round to visit their house in Glasgow. How embarrassed they were to realise they'd forgotten about the red ribbon with twenty world peace badges on it. How relieved when the woman told them that she was against nuclear weapons too.

John Kay was one of only two full-time Communist Party organisers in Scotland; his wife, Helen, shared his politics. I am not, nor have ever been, a Communist, but they sound like ideal parents. (Helen Kay doing the Christmas cards to the prisoners in South Africa: "Remember, it's not just Nelson.") I'd like to read more about them, and suggest to Kay that she could write a Marxist version of *Oranges Are Not The Only Fruit*. She demurs: perhaps optimistic, politically committed parents are harder to write about than pessimistic religious ones. Even though the party's long since over, it left its mark. All those socials for Chilean exiles after the CIA-inspired coup against Salvador Allende, all that defiant singing of *"Venceremos"*. "All those rallies. Marches against apartheid, miners'

The couple split up in 2005.

galas, *Morning Star* bazaars. The 'Free Angela Davis' poster on my bedroom wall. Reading about the Soledad brothers."

She's lived in Manchester for four years, but the first time she came she was just eleven. She can't remember the street, only that the red-brick terrace looked vaguely exotic after growing up in Bishopbriggs. They were all flying out to Yugoslavia, and the comrades put them up, same as they'd do anywhere. Visit London and you'd maybe stay with the Cohens, or the Huqs, a family of Indian comrades who called their son Pablo after Neruda (quite common among Indian Communists, she subsequently discovered). "Back in Glasgow, it was the same. We got meat from the party butcher every Saturday morning, half a pound of bacon and square sausages. If we needed a carpet put down, there'd be a party carpet fitter, there'd be a party plumber, party everything." Her parents' manifest faith in human nature had a downside though: as a child, Kay found there were things she couldn't tell them. At first, she didn't tell them about the bullying.

"Ten years ago, I'd still be angry at what happened. Now I'm not. I can't be bothered going on about it; I don't want to be forty and going on about children calling me names. But it still affects me, always will. If I pass a group of laughing kids, even now part of me still thinks they're laughing at me. There were three boys. They'd wait at the school gates and follow me. They would get some mud and wrap it up in sweet paper and say to me 'Do you want a sweet?' and I'd say no and they'd shove this mud in my mouth and two of them would hold me. The other one, they expelled him. His two friends were punished for three months each. Then I'd be walking along with my friends and they'd run up and say 'What do you call two darkies in a sleeping bag?' 'Twix.' 'What do you call a darkie that falls from a mountain?' 'Chocolate drop.' And (singing) 'Nuts oh hazelnuts, Cadbury's take them and they cover them with chocolate'. What I found excruciatingly embarrassing was that I was with friends. In a strange way, you felt you were embarrassing your friends. Yet I don't remember any of them ever sticking up for me, not the way my brother did. But it did all have some effect on me being a writer, because I'd go off and write these little poems of revenge. I was angry about other things too – apartheid, poverty. But that's how I started."

Something made that urge to write last longer than adolescent rage. Something deeper: a chain of ifs, of involuntary and voluntary choices. If she had known much more about her birth father than that he was a 5ft 6in Nigerian student of agriculture at Aberdeen University. If she had never wondered about her birth mother (at the time, they hadn't met). If she hadn't been bullied at school for the colour of her skin. If she hadn't nearly died in a motorcycle crash (something she's never mentioned to any journalist before). If she'd never loved her parents and been a Communist. If all of those things hadn't happened, perhaps she would never have been a writer. At seventeen, she still wasn't sure. A teacher referred her to Alasdair Gray, posted him her poems, sent her round. He opened the door to his flat in Kersland Street and said he'd read them and yes, she really is a writer. And she repeated that to herself all the way home, though she really didn't believe it yet. If anything, she thought, she was going to be an actress. So we need more ifs. If she hadn't loved women, perhaps. (She tells me she gave up on men when she was seventeen, and when I say that was a bit early she laughs her great big laugh and says that's nothing, she gave up meat when she was sixteen.) Want another ferret fact? Her last boyfriend was a dairy farmer in Dumfriesshire.

Cut to 1981 and Kay is reading English at Stirling. She's always read a lot, loves Burns and is working her way through the great African-Americans: Wright, Ellison, Baldwin, Alice Walker. She's always loved music too, maybe loved it even more than books: Count Basie and Ella Fitzgerald in concert on her fourteenth birthday; Bessie Smith, Pearl Bailey. Jazz. The blues. Call and response. The weight, the rhythm of words. Nearly there now. Was she confident enough by then, was that all it took to start writing? "It doesn't work like that. You need self-doubt when you write, but you also need self-belief. And it's a funny thing, because they are opposites. Too much self-confidence and you become arrogant about what you do, you learn what's successful and imitate it again and again. That's why I change forms such a lot."

There's ample evidence of her versatility. Next month sees the first of fifteen different productions of *Takeaway*, a play she has written primarily for young people. In September she'll be launching a children's book called *Strawgirl*, about a girl called Maybe Macpherson, whose father is Nigerian and mother Scottish, and who fights off three racist bullies on the Highland farm where she lives, with the help of a magical creature made out of straw. After that, there's another novel. She's still working on it, but it will be an imagined life based on an actress like Hattie McDaniel – you know, Scarlett's eye-rolling black servant in *Gone With the Wind*. "Everyone knows that woman, yet no-one knows that woman, and these apparent conundrums are what excite me – like in *Trumpet* how Joss (the lead character) seems to be a man but is in fact a woman. Nobody knows what she thought of when she went home at night, what she worried about in the morning, what she bought in the supermarket. Yet we know so much about all those other Hollywood stars, right down to how much they gambled and what kind of drugs they took. Right now, I'm trying to find an internal voice for her."

When she does, she'll write it in her attic study in the house she shares with Duffy and their two children in West Didsbury. In the House of Writers (five-bedroom, corner, by the River Mersey and off-limits to ferrets) Duffy's own study is on the ground floor. Kay's son, Matthew, is thirteen. She tells me two things about him. First, his name. When she was growing up, her favourite book was *Anne of Green Gables*. "I loved that book because she was adopted too. She had red hair and got picked on. But the father in that house was the kindest man, and he was called Matthew. So I called my son that because I wanted him to be kind too. And yes, he is.

Then she tells me the second thing. "He's a very good writer. My mum reads Matthew's stories and says: 'Listen. He's a lot better than you were at his age.' No, seriously!" And I laugh, because even ferrets like happy endings.

P.S. - *Jackie Kay's latest book is* **Darling: New and Selected Poems**, *published in paperback by Bloodaxe. Her four previous poetry collections* — **The Adoption Papers**, **Off Colour**, **Life Mask**, *and* **Other Lovers** — *are also available from Bloodaxe. Her short story collections* **Why Don't You Stop Talking** *and* **Wish I Was Here** *are both published by Picador, along with her novella* **Sonata**, *available in the Picador Shots series, and the novel* **Trumpet**. *Along with* **Strawgirl**, *her children's novel (published in paperback by Macmillan), Kay has also recently published a collection of poetry for children, which is available from Bloomsbury, with accompanying music CD.*

In 2006, Jackie Kay was awarded an MBE for services to literature.

Edwin Morgan

I first met him a fortnight after 9/11, when he was preparing to move out of the Anniesland flat in which he had lived for the previous thirty-nine years. He'd been diagnosed with prostate cancer (Doctor: "It could either be six months or six years" Morgan: "I'll have six years, please"), and was going to live in a nursing home. That's where I saw him again three years later, just after he had been appointed Scotland's first National Poet.

O N A TIDY desk in the middle of a tidy living-room in the tidiest of book-lined bachelor flats in Anniesland is a grey Adler typewriter. Edwin Morgan only uses it when he has already written out his poems in longhand. He cleans and services it every year. Every night he puts a cover on it. He's neat like that. And so is his poetry. No living poet is studied more widely in Scottish schools. His translations, from *Beowulf* to Mayakovsky, are internationally admired, his Scots *Cyrano de Bergerac* deeply loved. From the empathetic poetry of Glasgow social realism, his work swings out into concrete poetry, sound poetry, and some of the most penetrating poetic explorations of science and technology in the language. It sweeps across the millennia, usually towards the future. And though it plays profoundly, it never poses. Like its creator, it is both sparklingly intelligent and unassumingly friendly.

The following week Morgan has been invited to give the keynote reading at a poetry festival in St Andrews. On the cover of its programme there's a caricature of him throwing letters in an arc over his head like a juggler. Like Cinquevalli, he explains, referring to his poem about the famous Polish trapeze artist at the turn of the last century who, after a bad fall, practised juggling so determinedly that he could perform feats unequalled even now. When he died in Brixton, just before the Armistice, his coffin

...seems to burden the shuffling bearers, all their arms
cross-juggle that displaced person, that man
of balance, of strength, of delights and marvels,
in his unsteady box at last into the earth.

If any one of Morgan's poems had to stand for them all, he tells
me, this would be it. Why? He doesn't like to over-analyse the roots
of his poetry, but there's a clue right there. Wouldn't it be a hoot,
he is saying, if a loaded coffin were just a box of tricks, if the truly
balanced man, the juggler, really could overbalance Death? Already
he is the only survivor of the group immortalised in "Poets' Pub",
Sandy Moffat's famous portrait of the greats of twentieth-century
Scottish poetry: McCaig, MacLean, McDiarmid, Mackay Brown,
Goodsir Smith, Garioch, Morgan. But in those last four lines of
"Cinquevalli", he hints at the optimism that blazes through so much
of his poetry. We all know the coffin will inevitably go into the earth,
however much it seems to resist. And that is indeed the end: not for
Morgan the consolations of belief in an afterlife. Yet even here, on
the edge of nothingness, the skilful juggler's life still seems to be on
the verge of bursting out.

When I first met him, Morgan hadn't written any poems about
his illness. Later, when the cancer spread into his spine, making
walking impossible, leaving him in "quite a bit" of pain, he would.
When I visited him in his nursing home three years later, his book-
lined rooms had narrowed down to just a couple of shelves of books
and CDs (among them three Beatles albums, one by Tommy Smith,
two Shostakovich symphonies and Lou Reed's *Transformer*). On the
shelf beneath, in black and green-veined stone, was a 500-million-
year-old dinosaur egg. That mottled fossil provided him with a way
into the only poem he has ever written about cancer. "A lot of people think that cancer is relatively recent," he says, "but they've
found out that even dinosaurs had it. I hadn't wanted to write a
poem about cancer before, and this really isn't about my cancer, but
when I realised that it could take the form of a dialogue between a

normal cell and a cancerous one, and that this dialogue had been going on right back to pre-history, I felt as though I could handle it." The resultant poem, "The Sign of the Crab", includes a harrowing description of a cancer ward's midnight silence rent by the cries of a woman who had arrived too late see her dying husband, and another *"flapping and shrieking on the hospital bed / in what I imagine was very great pain"*. But for all his keen eye for suffering, Morgan soon spins his poem away from looking at it in individual detail. What's the point in concentrating on one person's pain among so many, he seems to be saying, especially when that genetic battle has taken such an massive toll all the way back to – well, to the time of the dinosaur egg on his bookshelf.

"The diagnosis was a real shock, to hear I had that taboo word, cancer. I had to just gradually get back to normal. But a couple of weeks after I wrote half a dozen poems that I think are quite good. They were about this change of life which I've got to get to grips with. One was about a gull that appeared on my window-sill. We don't get many of them here. But this gull looked inside for a long, long time, moved from leg to leg, and was looking at me, too. If I was superstitious, I'd say it was definitely an omen. I suppose I was just thinking when writing those poems, 'Well, this is where I live now, I'll be here for a few more years and what more will I see from my window?' One poem was about the clouds, another about rhododendrons out the front, another about the gasometer I can see from my kitchen window. Just poems about my life ..."

The way he says it, there's not a whiff of pathos. It's a matter-of-fact response, polite, direct. He went to hospital for a quarterly assessment a fortnight before we met and the hormone injection treatment seemed to be holding the cancer in check. "It's one of those cancers that may be there for a while – the doctors won't give you any prognosis – or it may hit you hard. All my doctor told me was that it would be between six months and six years. Well, I've had two and a half years so far, so I could go up to 85 if he's right.

I'm OK really. I just get tired, I'm not very good at travelling long distances or on stairs, but maybe that's just old age. I fell when getting off a bus last week. The thing is, when something like that happens, I have to be helped up. I can't do it by myself."

I think back to that great Morgan poem, "In the Snack-bar", now a set text on the Scottish Highers course, in which he writes about helping a blind man to go to the downstairs toilet and how afterwards

...he climbs
with many pauses but with that one
persisting patience of the undefeated
which is the nature of man when all is said.
And slowly we go up. And slowly we go up.
The faltering, unfaltering steps
take him at last to the door
across that endless, yet not endless waste of floor.
I watch him helped on a bus...

I think of that "undefeated", and of Cinquevalli's wobbling coffin, and I ask Morgan if he is an optimist. "Yes I am. I don't know where it comes from." An optimist with cancer? He smiles. "It's not your life that matters. It's what you do with it."

With hindsight, Morgan's life seems to have been predestined to poetry, though the writing came relatively late on: he was in his mid-forties when his first major book of poetry appeared. Before that, anything could have happened. When he was fourteen, for example, he nearly left school for a job as a carpet designer. Only because he took the road more travelled – staying on at school instead – do we have a poet who can dream up such delights as "The First Men on Mercury" or "The Loch Ness Monster's Song", rather than a man who can work out the number of whorls for a thick-pile Wilton. Even at that age, he knew he was gay. At first he thought it was just a phase. The received wisdom on homosexuality in the 1930s was that it was a disease for which the only cure was the love of a good woman. "It was hard to avoid feelings of guilt. Odd though it might seem, the army helped. It's very strange, but even in a war you can find that there are people like you – a lot more than I expected. It wouldn't be one in ten, more like one in thirty, say. Maybe it was more in the Medical Corps than it would have been elsewhere, I don't know."

Is it there, in the 42nd General Hospital, moving from Egypt to Lebanon and Palestine in the war years, that you look for the roots of his wide-ranging inventiveness? Or do you go further back, to a studious only child, voraciously reading science fiction in his parents' Rutherglen semi? Does his poetry owe anything at all to Glasgow University, to which, as a professor of English, he devoted his entire working life? How important was discovering Mayakovsky ? How much of his individuality lies in not having any gay role models or literary mentors? How is it that a man becomes such a balanced juggler with words? What's the trick?

Love has something to do with it. In 1963, Morgan met John Scott, a storeman from Law, near Carluke, in Lanarkshire, with whom he had a relationship that lasted for sixteen years, and ended only a year before Scott's death. Falling in love released some kind of creative flood in Morgan's poetry, which had been dammed up throughout the 1950s. For the first time, he said, he "had the confidence to write poems about anything at all". Love of Glasgow has something to do with it too. He's always lived in the city, choosing to stay there even when offered the chance of postgraduate study at Oxford. And as part of his job as Glasgow's Poet Laureate, he is now working on a series of long poems ("Operation Glasgow, I call it") about some of the people in the city's history. "Someone else said that in these poems there's a kind of coming together of my work, even though I'm not writing them about me. It gives me the chance to write in a way that is a kind of summing up."

Typically, there's not the remotest hint of civic worthiness about the project – the Glaswegians he unearths from history are a completely unpredictable bunch. Merlin, for one. "According to some authorities," says Morgan, "he lived at the court of King Roderick of Strathclyde in Dumbarton. He had a palace at Partick." Then there's Vincent Lunardi, the balloonist who was the first man to fly above Glasgow in the1780s; St Thennoch ("she was the mother of Glasgow's patron saint, St Mungo. St Enoch's Square should really be St Thennoch's Square: her remains are supposedly buried there, so it's holy ground"), and John and William Hunter, founders of the Hunterian Museum. Another on the list is Pelagius. "What do you know about him?" asks Morgan, leaning forward, eyes twinkling. "Only that he was a heretic," I reply. "Yes," he says, "all most people know of him is through him being denounced by St Augustine."

Later, I look up Pelagius on the internet, and I read that he was a fourth-century Briton who was essentially an optimist about humankind, which he thought untainted by original sin. That he was a man of great learning, who had travelled to Egypt and Palestine. "By some it is suggested," it concludes, "that his real name was Morgan."

P.S. - *At the time of writing, Edwin Morgan is 88. His most recent collection,* **A Book of Lives***, is available in paperback from Carcanet. Carcanet also publishes Morgan's* **Collected Poems***,* **Collected Translations***, and a paperback edition of his translation of* **The Play of Gilgamesh***. A selection of poems written by Morgan in response to art is published by Luath as* **Beyond the Sun: Scotland's Favourite Paintings***, and an edition of his translation of* **Sixty Poems of Attila József** *is published by Mariscat, which has also extensively published his poetry. There is a websited dedicated to Edwin Morgan at www.edwinmorgan.com, which also contains a full bibliography.*

Studs Terkel

A small bedroom in an unremarkable London hotel, and – unusually – I'm working with a freelance photographer I haven't never met before. The man staying there on a short publicity visit has been one of my heroes ever since I first read his books two decades ago. At the time of this interview, Studs Terkel is ninety, and plagued by deafness. When he switches his hearing aid to full volume the room is filled with an electronic hum, like you'd get from a small bank of amplifiers before the first chord is struck at a rock concert.

THE GREATEST Journalist in America is having his photograph taken. His London hotel room is tiny, and by the time the photographer has set up his lights and screens, there is no room to move. "Remember that Marx Brothers movie?" rasps Studs Terkel. "*A Night at the Opera?* The scene in the stateroom? All those guys crowded in?" Edged around the corner into the bathroom, I grin. "Could you stand up on the bed, Studs?" I hear the photographer say. The bed is a narrow single on casters: it glides across the carpet if you just nudge it. *Stand up on the bed? You've got to be joking! The guy is ninety years old!* is what I nearly say, what I should have said, what I wish I had said. But in the time it takes to not say that, I glance worriedly round the corner and he's already standing on the bed, wobbling but laughing. "You know, I was born in 1912," he says to the photographer. "The *Titanic* went down and I came up!" He puts on his pork pie hat and mugs for the camera. A showman. I never expected that.

Being the Greatest Journalist in America isn't about chasing exclusives. It isn't about celebrities, though Terkel has probably interviewed more people whose lives are really worth celebrating than anyone else on the planet. Slick insincerity, professional cynicism, unrestrained egotism – all the qualities that you'd expect to go with the title – for once don't apply. Being the Greatest

Journalist in America is about being the best person at listening to America, and for four decades, Terkel has been just that. While mainstream journalism all but ignored ordinary people, Terkel's ten books showed the extraordinary stories they were missing in the daily pursuit of celebrity. Taking Chicago as a template for America, but often ranging all over the country, his interviews provided proof of a seldom-tested thesis: that ordinary people's lives are indeed extraordinary. You want to know what it felt like to live through the Depression, you want to touch the shadow it cast across millions of lives, you read Terkel's interviews in *Hard Times* with the steelworkers it made redundant, or the farmers it forced out of Oklahoma. You want to find out what it was like to be black in Alabama before Rosa Parks got on that bus in Montgomery in 1955, you read Terkel's *Race*. The Pulitzer Prize came with *The Good War* in 1984, but the bestsellers had long preceded it. And at WFMT, the Chicago arts radio station where his daily show became a broadcasting legend, he had a free rein for forty-five years.

His new book, *Will the Circle Be Unbroken?*, is about death. Again, he went out on the road with his tape recorder to find out how a society with an ever-diminishing attention span was facing up to its one remaining taboo. Again, the stories he uncovers are compulsively readable and deeply moving. So here, for example, is a policeman rescuing a would-be suicide from a ledge at the top of one of the Twin Towers – a story Terkel was told six months before 9/11 – and thinking what a beautiful view he had of the East River as they swung out above it, both their lives in the balance, 110 storeys up. Here is a Hiroshima girl wondering where her mother is on 6 August, 1945. Threaded through all these memories are the kind of facts that you either don't know (that firefighters die eight to ten years younger than average) or forget about (how hair still blows in the wind, and the second hands on watches still spin round, even on corpses). This time, though, Terkel had an even greater empathy with his subjects. On 23 December, 1999, his wife Ida finally died after a long illness. They had been married for sixty years.

For such a gregarious, large-hearted man, Terkel is reticent about his private life. The people he talks to are the story, he insists; he isn't. He told his biographer Tony Parker that he had a mental block about telling Ida that he loved her, although he did. Ida was central to his life: the one who organised him, who drove him round America on interviews, who listened to all the other nine of his books as he read them to her. She liked that, because he read so well. It's the actor in him. They met when he was working on one of the federal relief programmes Roosevelt set up under the New Deal. "I remember this girl in a maroon smock, this very pretty, delicate girl. She and her black social worker friends would go into restaurants and people would say bad things and throw things at them. You know, she was one of the earliest protesting the Vietnam War, yet she's delicate, like a dancer. After she died, the poet Gwendolene Brooks said she could have danced on a moonbeam. So yes, writing this was a palliative. Every doctor I've ever met says, 'You gotta do this book,' because people don't want to talk about death, they only discuss it out of guilt and grief. But you should do it when you're healthy, because it's the most natural thing in the world. And this book is the most alive book I've ever done, because it makes you realise the preciousness of life."

The preciousness of life. That could be Doc Watson, the blind folk singer whose version of a gospel classic gives this book its title, talking about the death of his son Merle in a tractor accident. It could be the paramedics Terkel interviews, talking about breaking into rooms where people have died alone and looking at the photos on their walls. The New York firemen who smash through sixteen inches of brick wall to rescue eight of their trapped colleagues when the fire chief has told them they're wasting their time. But if you read Terkel's interviews closely, you start to notice a curious thing about them. Although they are about death, they are also flecked through with hope. A gay Chicago doctor has died of AIDS, but the lesbian mothers of his two sons fall in love. A man with incurable cancer makes a miraculous recovery after an out-of-body experience in which he imagines his three-year-old daughter finding him dead. A friend helps a black transvestite die with the kind of dignity the hospital authorities seem determined to deny her.

Death, in Terkel's stories from the streets, isn't always the end. It can elide into religious hope: the way the mother of fourteen-year-old Emmet Till – whose murder in 1955, because he had the temerity to whistle at a white woman, sparked the civil rights movement – looks at his broken body and thinks of Christ's agony; the way blind Doc Watson can still sing songs of praise to the God he believes is now caring for his dead son Merle. Although an agnostic ("a cowardly atheist") himself, Terkel still keeps an urn containing Ida's ashes on his windowsill. "I put yellow daisies next to it and keep them fresh, because I know she loves them," he says. "I don't put anybody down for whatever they believe. I don't mock anything that gives anybody solace." Terkel's books might provide some sort of solace too, for oral history also puts death's finality that little bit further back. The oral history of Terkel's own life takes him back to those 1920s nights when he listened outside Chicago's city-centre basement clubs to the sweet wafting notes of jazz and the haunting cries of the blues rising to the pavement; when he first heard the stories the working men told in his parents' rooming house; all the time drifting back to those distant years when the jobs in the city's stockyards and steel mills and the skyscrapers made it somewhere blacks in the South could look to as, in the words of one blues song, "a place called Heaven".

Finally, there is politics. These days, no-one looks there to find the kind of optimism that can expunge death's sting. But Terkel was a Roosevelt Democrat in the 1930s and, one suspects, still is. America, he says, has a "national Alzheimer's" about how the country was put back together by the New Deal. "Everyone forgets what big government did for our country when the religion they all worship now – free enterprise – fell on its fanny. The irony is that the very ones whose daddies and granddaddies' ass was saved by big government are the very ones who most condemn it now." How do you measure that optimism? In the definiteness of the "shall" in "We Shall Overcome", sung on the buses on the way to campaign against desegregation in Montgomery, Alabama, and on the train to Washington, to hear Dr King talk about his dream on the steps of the Lincoln Memorial. Terkel sang that song, took those buses, rode that train. He never sold out, even in the early 1950s, when he was one of America's first TV stars, and his refusal to kow-tow to McCarthyism cost him any hope of a job on the networks. Even in a new century, he's still kept his faith in what politics can do. One day, he imagines, an American President will come before the United Nations and echo Roosevelt's pledge to the poor in his second inauguration address in 1937 ("I see one third of the nation ill-fed, ill clothed, ill-housed") and apply it to the whole world. Unrealistic? Not if you're an optimist about human nature; not if you believe people can be redeemed. Terkel does, and to prove it, he tells me the story of how a Ku Klux Klan Grand Cyclops joined forces with a black woman who was organising a picket he helped to break up in Durham, North Carolina. Usually, he denies that he has any favourite interviews, he says, but really, that's the one.

He is lying down on the narrow hotel bed now, jetlagged from flying in that morning. The story spools into my tape recorder, as it once spooled into his. Like the actor he once was ("nearly always a dumb gangster in radio soaps"), he puts himself completely into all the roles. Even this tired, he's still the showman. He is, of course, far more than that. His hearing is going, his technological ineptitude is the stuff of legend. But his stories have all the sweep, all the emotion, and even more of the truth, than anyone could reasonably expect from even the Great American Novel. Here's part of one of them. Rick Rundle, a white man who works as a graffiti cleaner, has donated part of his liver to John Husar, a black journalist whom he knows from church. This is him talking, Terkel listening:

"When it's time for you to go, they say it's usually someone from the other world who you know who will come and get you. And not that I'd mind seeing my sister, who's been dead for twenty years or so — in that automobile accident. Or my father. But I see now that it'll probably be someone like John Husar.

"And in your mind, Studs, you would be at a radio station, doing a radio show of fifty years ago. And you would see someone that you haven't seen in a long time. And they'd say: 'Studs, where have you been? I've been looking for you. We've got another show to do on the other side of the river."

P.S. - *Since this interview, Studs Terkel's memoir* **Touch and Go** *has been published in hardback by The New Press. The New Press also publishes, in paperback,* **Race: How Blacks and Whites Think and Feel About the American Obsession, Working: People Talk About What They Do All Day And How They Feel About What They Do, Hard Times: An Oral History of the Great Depression, American Dreams: Lost and Found, Coming of Age: Growing Up in the Twentieth Century, Division Street: America,** *and* **The Studs Terkel Reader.**

Hope Dies Last: Making a Difference in an Indifferent World, And They All Sang: Great Musicians Talk About Their Music, *and* **Will The Circle Be Unbroken?** *are all available in paperback from Granta.*

The official website is at www.studsterkel.org. It is run by the Chicago Historical Society, and contains excerpts from his radio programmes.

Studs Terkel is now 95.

Epilogue: The Long Road Home

❖　　❖　　❖

I BEGAN this book in Kansas; I'll end it there too. I drive round to say my goodbyes to Clifford and Dolores Hope, walking up the path to their white-painted clapboard house, as Truman Capote and Harper Lee did on Christmas Day all those years ago. Up to the flyscreen door where, years later, Capote came back one morning to tell Dolores that a bunch of friends were gathering at his motel down the road, and that she just had to come and join them. He'd driven across from Kansas City in his Jaguar, which was parked on the road outside: they could go right away. Capote stood outside, pressing on the doorbell. Inside, Dolores had two small children to look after, another four due back from school, lunch cooking on the stove, and the phone was ringing. None of which registered with Capote, even when Dolores planted eighteen-month-old Rosemary firmly on his lap and told him that she just couldn't get away right now, Truman, she just couldn't.

I have nothing in common with Truman Capote, except that we both stood in front of the same doorbell with the same need: strangers in a strange town, wanting help with a story. But the difference is this: Capote *expected* it. His ego was that big, even before he'd written his masterpiece. Another example: the first time Capote visited the offices of the *Garden City Telegram*, at noon one day – the deadline for an afternoon newspaper – he barged into editor Bill Brown's office and demanded to speak to him. Brown told him he was too busy getting the paper out. The first time Capote talked to Alvin Dewey, the man leading the Clutter murder investigation, he antagonised him too. "Al sat down on him pretty hard," Dolores told me. "But that's why Nelle helped him so much. She smoothed the corners for him, and she wasn't there that day."

As I said at the start, in Kansas I'm just looking up footnotes of footnotes. But behind them all, there's something that matters. Or at least, it matters to me, because I still think that *In Cold Blood* is what journalism ought to aim at. That's why I'm in the Hopes' living room in Garden City, because the book their visitor went on to write – Dolores shows me her signed first edition – still echoes, decades later, in my mind. Any weaknesses in it, any gaps, are weaknesses and gaps in journalism; the trade in which I've worked all my life. As I leave, Clifford gives me a book, a memoir of his time as a GI in the Second World War, which he wrote after he retired. I put it on the front seat of my car and drive off to say goodbye to Duane and Orvileta West and to thank them for their help. Unlike Truman Capote, I never expected anyone to help me with this story: I rely on the kindness of strangers, but never take it for granted.

Truman Capote was just plain wrong about Duane West. Maybe he was wary of him: who else could have written a rival account of the Clutter murders better than the tall, handsome, 28-year-old who led the prosecution case against their killers? But I feel something like anger that Capote couldn't see what I see in West, and instead almost wrote him out of *In Cold Blood* altogether. Normally, I never mention whether or not I like the person I'm interviewing; usually, it's irrelevant. But I can't help liking Duane West, even though he doesn't make it easy for me. First he says he won't talk about Capote, then he says he will, but only if I pay $100 to a charity helping victims of the Greensburg hurricane. That's not how I work, I explain, but I can understand his reluctance to talk: why, after all, should his life be seen through the eyes of a writer who ignored him more than forty years ago? Doesn't everything else about his life count for far more: his faith, his years of service to Finney County, his enduring marriage, his four children? How can being slighted in literature outweigh all this? It can't – and nor does it stop him breaking out, at 76, in a starburst of new careers: he is the main agent for a Mexican artist who works entirely in cut cardboard, has plans to market Slice Cream (ice cream in a triangular carton), and is aiming to stage the musical he's just written about

Buffalo Jones, the founder of Garden City. This is a man with an enjoyably maverick mind; someone who thinks his own way through a problem, never mind the consensus. He describes growing up in Garden City so vividly that I can imagine the city growing up with him too. All the attentiveness I've given to *In Cold Blood*, all my own fascination with its background detail, is answered in West's conversation. It's a shame Capote never realised it.

But does the near-complete omission of West from *In Cold Blood* make it a lesser book? I don't think so. In the 1966 *New York Times* article in which he claimed to have invented the "non-fiction novel", Capote answered the charge. "I had to make up my mind, and move towards that one view, always," he wrote. "You can say that the reportage is incomplete. But then it has to be. It's a question of selection; you wouldn't get anywhere if it wasn't for that. I've often thought of the book as being like something reduced to a seed. Instead of presenting the reader with a full plant, with all the foliage, a seed is planted in the soil of his mind." He's right, of course. Prosecutor Works Hard to Convict Killers isn't a story; Killer Explains Senseless Murders is. All the emotional weight in Capote's story is taking you, not into the world as the regular inhabitants of south-west Kansas might experience it, but into the memories of two killers about to face the hangman's noose. The Duane Wests of this world are always going to feel cheated by journalism because a story picks its own path, and the familiar ruts of real life aren't always where it wants to go. So travelling to Kansas in search of Truman Capote was never going to be anything more than catching a few echoes of that story. The foliage of detail is still there, but the seed of the story has moved on, into the minds and memories of his readers. Yet there still was some point in going there: not just because of the story of the murder, horrific and senseless though it was, but because of where it had happened. Capote realised that small-town Kansas, so vastly different from his own Manhattan high society life, could not help but vivify his writing. "Everything would seem freshly minted – the people, their accents and attitudes, the landscape, its contours, the weather. All this, it seemed to me, could only sharpen my eye and quicken my ear."

As I followed in his footsteps, I felt that too. And never more so than when, just as I was leaving the Wests, Orvileta called me back. "Maybe you should listen to this," she said, and turned the radio volume up. It was a tornado warning. They're used to this in west Kansas: an urgent succession of beeps cuts into whatever radio programme people are listening to, and a metallic voice announces which way the tornado threat is coming. If there were a warning about incoming nuclear missiles, about the radioactive cloud drift patterns, this is how it would be voiced: in cold, sombre officialese, giving threat levels in the various affected counties across the state. After the beeps, the announcer reads the counties' names with deadpan precision: Haskell, Finney, Gray, Hodgeman... I'll be going through them on my way back east. In forty miles, I should hit the storm, which may or may not be accompanied by a tornado. Duane and Orvileta say I'm welcome to stay overnight with them if I want, but point out that it's not a full alert, just a warning of a possible tornado. Outside, the leaves are stirring and the clouds are slowly massing. We say our goodbyes, and I head east.

For the first ten miles, there's nothing. Then the rains come. The sky darkens and lightening flashes, at first so faint and distant that I wonder whether I might have been imagining it. Through the deluge, I latch onto an orange school bus ahead, and try to keep focusing on it through the futile swish of the windscreen wipers. For mile after mile, I follow the bus, then it turns off to the left, and I am alone on the prairie, the sky now black above me, the rain shrinking perspective, bringing the limits of my vision impossibly close. I drive on, through that thirty-mile carwash, and because I can't see the horizon I start wondering whether I'm travelling uphill or downhill, even though my brain tells me that the road I'm driving on is as flat as, well, Kansas. Then the storm passes and the horizons widen to their normal yawning immensity. I stop the hired car, get out and smoke a cigarette, and smell the freshness of the new-washed fields. Getting back in, I notice Clifford's war memoir lying on the passenger seat. I'll read that, I promise myself, as soon as I possibly can. And I head onwards, the hundreds and hundreds of miles to home.

❖   ❖   ❖

As far as I know, the only memoir anyone in my family has ever written is about war too, although memoir is probably too grand a name for my grandfather's neat copperplate account of being at Passchendaele in the First World War. And as I set out on one last journey along the line between fact and fiction, that's where I'll begin, in a nightschool notebook sent to me recently by a relative who was clearing out her house.

We're a small family, barely extended, and none of the last century's wars killed any of us. In every war we were asked to fight, we fought, but not with conspicuous heroism: our family's inlaid parquet box of medals are all for taking part, not for valour. Their rainbow silk is starting to fade, their pins beginning to rust, and the strange, soldierly faces in the photos gradually blending to a dull, uniform khaki. But the medals themselves are still clear; and round the edge of one – a silvery disc showing a naked horseman trampling over a skull and crossbones – is the name of the combatant to whom it was awarded: *40417 Cpl G Robinson R Dub Fus.* Greenwood Robinson. Such an English name. My grandfather. Greenie, we called him. Who was he?

I remember a kindly man, a gentle Yorkshire mill-worker, whom my sister and I loved because he gave us more sweets than anyone else in the family. He used to lift us up and pretend to stick us to walls. Then he'd look down and ask us what we'd done with his fingers. We used to scream with delight, because on his right hand three of them were missing.

It happened in 1917 – but how, I never found out. No-one

seems to have asked him whether he shot them off himself, as some soldiers did when the horrors got too much. My sister says she'd heard it happened when he fired a rifle round a corner. Certainly, he was honourably discharged: on 21 November 1917, the day he left the army, his colonel noted that he was "a very good man, had served his country well and was wounded in its defence". I only ever saw him cry once. We were watching the 1965 Remembrance Day service from the Albert Hall on TV. That bit where a million poppies floated down from the ceiling, one for every man killed. *Abide with me, fast falls the eventide*. Tears rolled unstoppably down his face. Why? I wondered as a child. What had he seen?

Three decades later, his notebook gave me the answers – or rather, part of the story. Take, for example, rats. As we know from just about every other account, the trenches were infested with both black and brown varieties. The corpses, piled three or four deep in no-man's land, kept the rats fed so well that they became gourmands, disdaining all but the tastiest parts of the human body, the eyes and liver. In winter, when lulls in fighting reduced the supply of fresh corpses, rats would attack sleeping men and the wounded. But Greenie's angle on the subject of rats is an object lesson in Victorian detachment and English understatement. "Vermin," he notes, "were Tommy's greatest enemy."

At Passchendaele, he was in Z Company of the 1st Royal Dublin Fusiliers. By 1916, the tide of Irish history had already challenged the idea of Irish soldiers fighting in British uniforms, and after the Easter Rising, those soldiers began to look less like heroes and more like traitors to their compatriots. So, when German machine-guns on the Somme winnowed their ranks still further, there were no new Irish recruits; and since Ireland was too volatile to impose conscription, the gaps were filled by British soldiers. By people like Greenie, who had arrived in France with the Tyneside Irish. It was his first time away from his mother country, as he always called it, and he was missing his old life. Herded on to the ships at

Folkestone, marching endlessly in the soft sand at the British base at Étaples, where tents stretched for as far as the eye could see, crammed into wagons on the slow-moving trains to the front, he wasn't impressed. "A captain once told me that a man only made a number," he wrote, "and I have lived to prove his words." Still, that summer was hot, and at Z Company's first billet they could fish in a stream and relax in the shade of an orchard. In the French villages they marched through, the only people Greenie saw were old, and he wondered if they had pensions like the one Lloyd George had introduced back home. Summer passed and the weather turned wet. Moving up from the reserve trenches to the front, "I saw sights I do not wish to remember or tell". After going back to get more rations, he returned to find his company wiped out by a direct hit.

And so to Passchendaele, one of the most hellish battles of a hellish war, not least because it took place in a sea of mud. On the night before the big push, Greenie was making his way back to the trenches when got lost next to a military cemetery, with hundreds of wooden crosses in the ground. They'd have been arranged in lines once, but heavy shelling had blown the shallow graves, dug only to a spade's depth, wide open. "At least it was night," he consoled himself, "but the smell was unbearable." He doesn't write about the horrors he saw there, or when he went over the top. He doesn't talk about the burial details, stumbling through the mud on double rum rations, putting bodies in graves that flooded immediately in what was to become Britain's largest military cemetery. He doesn't describe death or suffering; his phrases are shrouds, or evasions. "You can imagine our distress".

I can't think of Greenie's memoir without also returning to Sebastian Barry's 2005 novel *A Long, Long Way*. It, too, deals with the Royal Dublin Fusiliers, but this time from an Irish point of view. And Barry imagines every last bit of the distress that soldiers like my grandfather experienced: the full horrors of the gas attack, in which hundreds of them died, only eight days after the Easter Rising back in Dublin; the steady thinning of the ranks thereafter, the growing sense of doom, and – for the Irishmen in the regiment – the further tragedy of being trapped on the wrong side of their own country's history, alienated from friends and family by the uniform in which they fought.

A Long, Long Way was shortlisted for the 2005 Man Booker Prize. It is a beautifully realised, intensely moving novel – but its cultural significance extends far beyond its literary achievement. By imagining, so fully, this moment of history, from this perspective, Barry has changed the present. Before this novel, the hundreds of thousands of Irish who fought for Britain in the two World Wars were at best unremembered, and at worst attacked and spat upon every Remembrance Day; their sacrifice ignored by historians and left in an enduring no-man's land. What *A Long, Long Way* did, in effect, was to bring these old soldiers back into the fold of a new, more inclusive Irishness. The Ireland I remember from living there in the early 1980s – friendly, but inward-looking and hypocritical – would have had no time for the Royal Dubs; the new Ireland remembers them. Sebastian Barry, in other words, hasn't just transformed the story of men like my grandfather into fiction; he's taken it a long, long way further than that. Like Capote's *In Cold Blood*, he has created a seed for the imagination that will outlive our memory of those it describes.

❖   ❖   ❖

The line where fact and fiction meet runs through only a few of the books discussed in these interviews. For some novelists, the very notion that their fiction is anything to do with their own lives is absolute heresy: to suggest it is as jejune as asking "Where do you get your ideas from?" Others accept, with Graham Greene, that writers gives something of themselves away every third sentence, and secretly wonder whether it's really more often than that. With many, you can see the life in the work like the reflection of a fallen log over a fast-running stream: not a clear reflection, but unignorable all the same. However the seed is formed – that thing that makes fiction adhere to the reader's mind – doesn't matter half as much as the seed itself.

Through my job as books editor of *The Scotsman,* I've been privileged to meet some of the most dazzlingly imaginative writers alive. My admiration for them is only enhanced by my – fortunately early – realisation that I couldn't do what they can. I was eighteen, and had just got some sort of grant to go on a creative writing class run by the Arvon Foundation. Arvon has been going now for forty years, but this was in the early days, at Lumb Bank, the eighteenth-century mill-owner's house high above Heptonstall in West Yorkshire, where Ted Hughes had once lived. The week-long course was taught by Stan Barstow, author of the 1960 novel *A Kind of Loving* – now all but forgotten, but then still very much part of mainstream literary culture in the north of England. I remember being impressed by him, because he was the first novelist I'd ever met – but my memory draws a merciful veil over whether or not I wrote anything; if I did, whether I read it out; and if I did that, what everyone else thought of it.

My clearest memory is that a journalist from the *Yorkshire Post* came to write a feature on the group. Creative writing courses hardly existed back then, so I suppose we must have been newsworthy. He arrived at the end of the week and sat in on the discussion. The group had got on well, and as it was a scorching June day, we were all sitting outside in the front garden. After a couple of hours, the journalist stood up and made his excuses. He'd asked all the questions he needed to, and now he'd better get back to the office. Oddly, although I can barely remember a single other thing about that week, I can recall the next ten seconds as though they were happening now. Barstow, bearded and red-shirted, sitting seigneurially in a rocking chair in the sun, waving a warning hand at the journalist as he walked down the front path towards his car. The heat haze in the steep valley behind him. And then the shouted words at the journalist's retreating back came with that warning: "Hey lad! Make sure you tell it like it is! Tell it like it is, lad, right?"

We all laughed, the rest of us in that group sitting out in the sun, because none of us was a journalist. Yet now I think of that impossible advice almost every time I sit in front my computer to write up an author interview.

Tell it like it is, lad. Right?